MW01156964

THE SHOT

Watson, Nicklaus, Pebble Beach,
and the Chip That Changed Everything

CHRIS MILLARD

Foreword by Tom Watson

Introduction by David Fay

BACK NINE PRESS

Back Nine Press
Chicago, Illinois
www.back9press.com
Instagram and X: @backninepress

Portions of this text previously appeared in the June 14, 2010, edition of *Golf World* Magazine and appear here with the permission of *Golf Digest*.

9 8 7 6 5 4 3 2 1
First Edition
Printed in China

Library of Congress Control Number: 2024944904
The Shot: Watson, Nicklaus, Pebble Beach, and The Chip
That Changed Everything
Written by Chris Millard

Back Nine Press (USA)
Pages cm
ISBN: 978-1-956237-25-2 (hardback)
ISBN: 978-1-956237-27-6 (ebook)

For the late, great Terry Galvin

CONTENTS

FOREWORD

FROM THE TIME I COULD HIT a golf ball, I had my heart set on winning a U.S. Open. Maybe my upbringing had something to do with that. I was raised in a traditional, Midwestern household where the Pledge of Allegiance, church, and sports were the mainstays of our daily life. My dad always referred to our national championship not as the U.S. Open, but as the National Open. That's old school, and it resonated with me. It was a way of making the championship sound as regal as it truly is.

In my youth, dinner-table conversation was often centered on U.S. Open trivia, such as who won in a given year, on what course, and over whom.

All of that bred in me a deep passion for that championship. Of course, passion can be a funny thing. Sometimes, the more you revere something, the more you crave it, the less attainable it seems. And as much as I hungered for a U.S. Open title, several of my early chances slipped right though my fingers. In 1974, I led the U.S. Open at Winged Foot after 54 holes. I shot 79 on Sunday to tie for fifth. Sure, I won some tour events: I won the British Open in my first appearance in 1975. I won the 1977 Masters over Jack Nicklaus, and I beat Jack again in the 1977 British Open at Turnberry. I was winning tour events; I was winning majors; I was even beating the best player who'd ever played the game, but I was 0-fer the U.S. Open.

That all changed in June of 1982. Eleven years after turning professional, I won my beloved U.S. Open—er, National Open. I beat Jack Nicklaus. I did it on a golf course that both he and I believe to be one of the finest in the world. I won the championship of the United States, and to top it all off, I did it on Father's Day. I've had my share of competitive thrills, but I can say that winning the 1982 U.S. Open under those conditions was the biggest thrill of my sporting life.

Chris Millard has taken the elements that made that week so special and memorable for me, and has woven them with his own research and insights into the history of the course, the remarkable life of the 17th hole, and the DNA of this great championship. He has an entire chapter dedicated to one little chip shot, as well as some fascinating revelations on the broadcast of that event and how it changed television history. As Chris says, after that week everything changed, nothing was the same. That was especially true for me.

—Tom Watson

INTRODUCTION

THE FIRST TIME I EVER SET FOOT on the Monterey Peninsula was in 1971. I was 20 years old, and as I drove down 17-Mile Drive, I realized that not only was I passing directly through the hallowed grounds of Cypress Point, but I was within a few feet of the 15th tee (the 16th hole gets all the attention, but 15 is a stunner of a par three). So, I did what any self-respecting golf nut would have done: I put the car in park, popped the trunk, pulled one club and one scuffed ball from my bag, and played a furtive shot into the idyllic 15th green. I think I was back in the car and scrambling away before the ball even hit the ground.

That innocent little trespass illustrates in some ways the arc of my career. I grew up caddying—the blue-collar guy in the white-collar world—and then spent some 32 years at USGA, 20 of them as executive director. It was a Zelig-like career, in which I found myself at the game's most iconic venues, rubbing shoulders with the greatest players of all time, and immersing myself in in the history of the game. A quick example: Some of you might recall that the 1-iron Hogan made famous in via his win in the 1950 U.S. Open was stolen after that championship. Through a circuitous series of sales of the club in 1983, it ended up where it belonged—in the USGA Museum. I was able to confirm the authenticity of the club and the bizarre story around it in a phone call with Mr. Hogan himself. A few years later, NBC which was telecasting a USGA Championship and asked if we might bring the club to the set and make the Hogan 1-iron available to the TV audience. I promised them it would be there. In fact, the storied club made the trip from my home in New Jersey to the Philadelphia area in my golf bag—14-club rule be damned—and the night before I brought it to the Open, a Philly friend and I surreptitiously hit balls with it from his lawn onto the campus of neighboring Bryn Mawr College. I've since presumed that our collective shot dispersion was slightly wider than Mr. Hogan's.

Anyway, since 1971 I've been out to Pebble several times, both for fun and for work (if you can call it that). In fact, I may have had the best seat in the house for the 1982 U.S. Open. As detailed later in this book, I was a young USGA staffer in 1982. My only job on that particular Sunday was as the starter. All I had to do was correctly announce the names of the contestants and their hometowns to the galleries and the fans watching at home. Once I'd dispatched all the contestants, I had nothing much left to do. So, I joined my friend Tom Meeks in the scoring tent by the 18th hole, a little tent which happened to command a majestic view of Stillwater Cove. The players would come up 18, enter the booth, commiserate over their play, and sign their cards. As they processed through the tent, I was the proverbial fly on the wall for one of the seminal moments in our centuries-old game. (You can read all about it in Chapter 13).

Having attended that U.S. Open and at least 20 more since, I will say that the 1982 U.S. Open is certainly in the top two or three of all U.S. Opens, and that's only because I'm really trying to be fair and save room for that forgotten Open that could possibly make a case for being Number 1. In 1982 you had Nicklaus, who had already won four U.S. Opens, hoping to surpass Wille Anderson, Bobby Jones and Ben Hogan to become the only player ever to win five; who for most of his life has declared that if he had one round left to play it would be at Pebble Beach; who had won the U.S. Amateur at Pebble in 1961 and who had won the U.S. Open there in 1971, courtesy of another of the great 1-irons in all of golf history.

As hard as it is to imagine, Tom Watson's ties to Pebble, while not as epic, were certainly deep and maybe even just as emotional. To understand them you have to have known Frank "Sandy" Tatum. Tom had a terrific dad in Ray Watson, but he also had a second father—maybe not a godfather, let's call it a golf-father—in Sandy Tatum. Ray got Tom into the game, but it was fellow Stanford alum Sandy who instilled in Watson a love for links golf. In fact, it was their trips to Scotland and Ireland that instilled in Tom a passion for the odd bounces, respect for both good and bad breaks, and the creativity required become the greatest (British) Open champion of modern times.

On top of that, as relayed in this book, during his college days at Stanford, Tom made frequent dawn patrol trips from Palo Alto to Pebble, where his friendship with the starter, Ray Parga, led to more than a few off-the-tee-sheet practice rounds. We all played those late afternoon putting and chipping games as kids: *"If I hole this, I beat Nicklaus for the Open title."* The only difference between Tom and the rest of us was that Tom was doing it at Pebble, and the part about beating Jack actually happened.

Juxtapose all that with the frustration Watson had to be feeling in 1982. I've never asked Tom this question, but I think I know the answer. If Watson had to surrender all of his major championship titles, but could only keep one, I think he'd keep the U.S. Open trophy. Maybe that's my USGA bias, but knowing Tom and his deep affection for and pride in his country, I think the U.S. Open towers above his other accomplishments. But remember that he came to Pebble in June of 1982 having never won the U.S. Open title he craved, while his most celebrated opponent already had four.

Not only was it Jack and Tom, but it was Pebble, which in my estimation is either the Number 1 or 2 golf course in the world, the only other contender being the Old Course at St Andrews. The fact that Pebble—a relative newcomer, a piker, to the game—can even give the ancient Old Course a run tells you what a spectacular golf course it really Is. Pebble arrived on American golf's radar in 1929 when it hosted the U.S. Amateur. But like virtually every other facet of American life, golf and Pebble took a hit during the Great Depression and struggled right on through World War II. It was Bing Crosby's fabled Clambake, which first visited Pebble in 1947, that put Pebble on the modern golf map. This means that in 2024, Pebble has only been truly known to the golf world for 77 years. The Old Course has been around, depending on who you ask, for 500 or 600 years. That's how good Pebble is.

This book is like a reunion for me; it makes me feel young again while reminding me that I'm not. Forty-two years after Watson's win this beautiful book brings back in living color so many of the details that might have been lost to history had they not been so thoughtfully collected by my friend, Chris Millard. From the founding days of the USGA to the design evolution of Pebble, to the make, model, and (stunning) provenance of the sand wedge that Watson used to play the shot, I'm delighted to see this book in the hands of people who have as much reverence as I do for both Pebble Beach and the 1982 U.S. Open.

—David B. Fay

PREFACE

"AND HE'S OVER. INTO THE DEEP STUFF."

Jim McKay was sitting in a broadcast booth at Pebble Beach Golf Links. The avuncular everyman of ABC Sports, whose nasal folksiness had rendered him narrator-in-chief of American sport, was eyeing the action on a television monitor. Some 500 yards away, Tom Watson, claimant to five major championships—but never the U.S. Open he coveted—was deadlocked with Jack Nicklaus for the 1982 edition.

Watson's 2-iron tee-shot had roosted in the wispy rough left of the 17th green. Not only had Watson missed the putting surface, he had done so on the short side. Only deep grass and about 12 feet of slick green—all downhill—remained between his ball and the hole. Bogey—or much worse—had entered the equation, and Watson's chances of capturing this U.S. Open, or perhaps any U.S. Open, seemed doomed.

CHAPTER 1

The Open Blossoms

IT WAS THE EARLY 1890s and the nascent American game was in chaos. Various clubs were promoting their own "national championships." Chicago's Charles Blair Macdonald, then among the best and most knowledgeable players in the U.S., offered a solution.

His argument for a sanctioning body overseeing the American game resounded with Henry O. Tallmadge, a member at St. Andrew's Golf Club in Yonkers, Theodore A. Havemeyer of Newport, and Laurence Curtis of The Country Club. With their own plans for a sanctioning body already forming, the trio grew concerned that an alienated Macdonald might combine his stature in the game with his midwestern connections and form his own organization. Shortly thereafter, on December 22, 1894, Tallmadge hosted a New York dinner attended by representatives of St. Andrew's, Newport, The Country Club, Shinnecock, and Macdonald's Chicago Golf Club. They would create the Amateur Golf Association of the United States, the short-lived forerunner of today's United States Golf Association. Its mission has since sprawled into Rules, handicapping, the Golf Handicap Information Network (GHIN), turfgrass research and consulting; an equipment research and test center; regional and sectional affairs; a museum; a members program; a charitable arm and even corporate sponsorship deals, but the mission to which a handful of men agreed that night at the tony Calumet Club on the northeast corner of Fifth Avenue and 29th Street, was simple: "to promote the interests of the game of golf, to promulgate a code of rules for the game, and to hold annual meetings at which competitions shall be conducted for the amateur and open championships of the United States of America."

The newborn U.S. Open might have been expected to ascend quickly to a position as the nation's premier championship. Not so. For years the Open lagged far behind the U.S. Amateur in prestige. The very wording of the USGA's mission statement revealed the primacy of the Amateur (" ... to hold annual meetings at which competitions shall be conducted for the amateur and open championships of the United States of America"). For further evidence, consider the inaugural USGA championship slate: The first sanctioned U.S. Amateur Championship was contested at Newport on October 3, 1895—one day before the first sanctioned U.S. Open. Thankfully, for those who had had enough of his boorishness, C.B. Macdonald won that Amateur title.

The first U.S. Open—a figurative afterthought—was staged the following day. The Open's second-class status reflected society's disdain for professional sportsmen and the not entirely inaccurate consensus that professionals of the era were ill-mannered, distasteful, and intemperate money-grubbers. Fittingly, the first player to tee off in that down market championship wasn't even a competitor, but a marker by the name of E.C. Rushmore who was filling in for a no-show. The winner was Horace Rawlins, who beat an elfin Scot named Willie Dunn by two shots.

This is how the Open hobbled along for much of its young life, an interloper's picnic dominated by expat Brits and Scots who had settled in the United States. That would soon change.

If the U.S. Open in particular and the sport in general needed a hero, he arrived in the spindly, mild-mannered form of 20-year-old ragamuffin Francis Ouimet. Ouimet's father was a laborer, a gardener at The Country Club. He had a sweat-soaked disdain for the pastimes of the idle rich. Still, the family's proximity to the club and the resulting ability of his sons Francis and Wilfred to earn money there, gave the father some solace. Ouimet—who is described in his World Golf Hall of Fame citation as having stepped "from the pages of a Dickens novel"—began caddying at TCC at the age of 11. He and his brother Wilfred, also a caddie, took the game home, somehow getting their hands on a forlorn golf club and digging three "holes" in the family's yard. Nine years later, in 1913 at the age of 20, Ouimet won the hotly contested Massachusetts Amateur and decided to enter the Open, which was being contested across the street from his ramshackle home. In an outcome that still stuns logic, the fresh-faced caddie, unknown outside his state, with a 10-year-old street-smart kid named Eddie Lowery on his bag, turned back the world's two finest golfers—Harry Vardon and Ted Ray—in a three-way playoff to win the U.S. Open.

Ouimet's win remains the greatest upset in U.S. Open history—for that matter, in all of golf history. Even the *New York Times*, which hadn't seen fit to cover much early American golf, ran the Ouimet story on the front page: the first time the game had enjoyed such rarified real estate. The *Times* piece, written by Henry Leach (a Brit, interestingly), conveyed the flabbergasting quality of Ouimet's accomplishment:

"When we have discovered perpetual motion, when we know the secrets of life after death, and when we may go for weekend trips to Jupiter and Mars—perhaps then I will believe that your little Francis Ouimet has won today. This was the greatest day in all golf history. There will never be another like it. There can't be."

Ouimet's win was an ad man's dream. It was, in essence, the original USGA "For the Good of the Game" PSA. And it hit home. In 1913, roughly 350,000 Americans were playing golf. A decade later, that number was up to 2 million.

If Ouimet gave the Open its open-ness; if he animated the everyman American qualities that had lain dormant in the Championship, then seven years later, another beloved amateur would refine the Open, smooth its edges, and lend it a touch of class and southern gentility. He would also give it staying power.

The accomplishments of Muhammad Ali, Pele, Michael Jordan, and Tiger Woods are extraordinary, but none holds a candle to the celebrity that shined on Robert Tyre Jones Jr. in the 1920s. The media world has changed immeasurably in the last 80 years. All-sports cable networks, satellite services, wireless communications, and, of course, the Internet, have stepped up the pace at which a global image can be created, sustained, embellished, or demolished, but if one was able to measure the excitement (not the audience) generated by one athlete over a given period of time, Jones is virtually untouchable. In fact, Jones' impact may best be appreciated when looked at in retrospect. More than nearly a century after his last victory and more than 50 years after his death, Bob Jones remains part of the everyday fabric of his game. Aside, perhaps, from Babe Ruth, no other athlete can make that anachronistic claim. Jones' exploits, his swing, his grace and even his foibles are still the stuff of weekend four-ball conversations, broadcast commentary and sports-page editorials. He's virtually kin to the generations of golfers who followed. The man who referred to himself as "Bob" and whose closest family and friends used that name, is still known around the golfing world by the endearing nickname, Bobby.

Jones not only became America's most celebrated athlete, he did so during the 1920s, the so-called "Golden Age of American Sports." On a daily or weekly basis, the ink-stained wretches of the then vastly influential American print media had a veritable buffet of worthy headliners from which to choose. Ruth, Rockne, Grange, Dempsey, and Tilden dominated their sports. Horseracing, in its heyday in the 1920s, was blessed with the beauty and dominance of Man O' War, the greatest horse who ever lived. Jones played a game less popular than any of the above, yet he easily wrested the 1920s from all of them and, remarkably, he did so as an amateur— a part-time golfer and a full-time lawyer. In fact, one can argue that the esteem in which amateur athletes were held in the early 20th century owed much to Jones' personal celebrity.

Jones owned the era, winning the more prestigious U.S. Amateur five times. And when he began to win U.S. Opens (1923, 1926, 1929, and 1930), his enormous personal popularity lent credence, even significance, to that championship. He might as well have dipped it in bronze. The peak for Jones (and for American amateur sport) would come in 1930 when Jones captured the Grand Slam—U.S. Open, U.S. Amateur, British Open, and British Amateur— a feat never duplicated. Today we recognize celebrity by bestowing an Oscar, signing an endorsement deal, or publishing a grim mug shot on the cover of *People* magazine. In the first half of the 20th-century there was no greater recognition than a ticker tape parade down New York City's Canyon of Heroes. Jones remains the only solo athlete ever to receive multiple Fifth Avenue parades; In 1926 for becoming the first player to win the U.S. and British Opens in the same year, and in 1930 for completing in one year what sportswriter George Trevor of the *New York Sun* termed "The impregnable quadrilateral."

The headline-grabbing U.S. Open victories by Ouimet and Jones formed the foundation of the U.S. Open's enduring significance. By the time Jones retired from the game in 1930 at the age of 28, the U.S. Open, once regarded as a low-class undercard to the Amateur Championship, had emerged as the elite title in American golf. The great players who migrated to the Championship during Jones' self-described "fat years" continued to compete after his departure from the stage. By drawing the greatest players in the world to the toughest courses in the United States, the Open had become one of the yardsticks used by historians, writers, and players in the determination of greatness. By definition, virtually every great American player since Jones has won at least one U.S. Open: Hagen, Sarazen, Nelson, Hogan, Casper, Nicklaus, Palmer, Player, Trevino, Miller, Watson, and Woods. Of the premier players in American history only two—the late Sam Snead and Phil Mickelson—never hoisted the Open trophy (although both players combined for an agonizing 10 runner-up finishes.

CHAPTER 2
California Dreaming

IN THE FALL OF 1927, the USGA announced that it would bring the 1929 U.S. Amateur to Pebble Beach. It had been known for some time that the Association was interested in bringing the Amateur to California, which had begun to emerge as both an economic power and a celebrity playground. Given Pebble's rising stature as a gathering place for vacationing easterners and even a residence for transplanted socialites, the selection made sense. Early American golf courses and championships were raggedy affairs with none of the grooming and polish associated with today's game. The USGA, founded in 1894, was still young, but the move to the westernmost reaches of the Union made a bold statement about American interest in the sport, and as the game leaped westward it revealed its ambitions. A bulked-up Pebble Beach awaited those who made the pilgrimage. *The New York Times* presaged the stern challenge that Pebble would ultimately present: "Plans will be set into motion at once to stiffen it up for the 1929 onslaught."

Pebble Beach may be anchored to the rocky shores of Monterey, but its genealogy traces to 1869, a peak in Utah and, most directly, the evolution of the Iron Horse. Said less poetically, the golf course that set the American standard for beauty and difficulty was essentially founded as a tourist trap.

Only four years after the publication of the Emancipation Proclamation, four California-based entrepreneurs, Charles Crocker, Leland Stanford, Collis Huntington, and Mark Hopkins, led the completion of the Trans-Continental Railway with the driving of the "Golden Spike" at Promontory Point. Eleven years later and more than a century before the phrase entered popular lexicon, these capitalist Californians subscribed to the theory that "if you build it, they will come." Their newly formed (and audaciously named) Pacific Improvement Company opened the Hotel Del Monte near Monterey. Thanks to the westward reach of the Southern Pacific Railroad, guests in search of the curative ocean breezes of Northern California could now arrive at the Monterey Peninsula via the newly christened "Del Monte Express."

There they could sit in the Hotel Del Monte, look out on to Stillwater Cove, and see why renowned author Robert Louis Stevenson famously described this coastal paradise as "this most felicitous meeting of land and sea." Or not. Turns out Stevenson never said it. The actual author of those words was a local artist by the name of Francis McComas. In fact, the quote was not even about Pebble Beach but about nearby Point Lobos, which is visible from Pebble (more about McComas later).

Such myths are sewn into the fabric of Pebble Beach. Mythology, more cynically described as long-term hype, is one of the defining characteristics of great American institutions. Pick an American icon—George Washington, the Yankees, Hollywood—each is a product of decades or centuries of myth piled warmly on fact and served lovingly to consumers. Like the swollen lip of a greenside bunker that rises with every splash-out, these myths grow so large that they eventually become the thing itself, which is convenient, because it's what the people really want anyway.

Pebble Beach is the perfect example. As unified as the course is with the ground and as naturally as it lays beside the sea, the history of Pebble Beach—how world-class golf arrived and thrived here—is as circuitous, unnatural, odds-defying, and fact-challenged as it gets. Herbert Warren Wind once wrote, "Pebble Beach really is one of golf's happiest accidents." He was exactly right.

The ass-backwards happenstance quilt that is Pebble's history dates to the very claiming of Northern California for the United States. That monumental step in America's westward expansion actually came in 1846 courtesy of an eastward-bound Navy vessel under the command of Commodore John Drake Sloat, who entered the harbor at Monterey on July 2, 1846. Four days later he sent a dispatch to a colleague that read in part, "I have determined to hoist the flag of the United States at this place tomorrow, as I would prefer being sacrificed for doing too much than too little."

The land on which Pebble Beach Golf Links now sits has seen numerous owners since the 1800s. In the 1820s, when the Mexican influence in the region began to recede, the land, then known as "El Rancho Pescadero," was controlled by the Carmen Barreto family. In 1840 the 4,000 seaside acres were sold to a Mr. John Romie for $500. Romie sold the parcel in 1853 to John Gore who, in turn, would lose the property in a sheriff's sale in 1862. The buyer turned out to be a son-in-law of Romie, a Scots-born New Englander by the name of David Jacks.

In his book *Pebble Beach Golf Links: An Official History*, Neal Hotelling says that Jacks was a major player in the area's real estate dealings, at one time or another buying or selling "nearly every piece of land in Monterey County." But Jacks was simply a dealmaker. He had no particular vision for Pebble Beach's future. In fact, it wasn't until the creation of the Pacific Improvement Company (PIC) that Jacks even had the ingredients for a profitable flip: a buyer with both money and dreams.

In 1880 Jacks sold to PIC two ranches incorporating what is now the Del Monte Forest, most of Pacific Grove, and parts of Carmel. Shortly thereafter, in June of 1881, PIC opened scenic 17-Mile Drive. The winding coastal road that gave travelers unmatched seaside vistas and led—unsurprisingly—directly to the Hotel Del Monte, where luxury rooms abounded and even as early as the late 1890s, the game of golf awaited.

Today, the golf course at Pebble Beach enjoys such a high profile that most casual fans are not even aware of the fact that long before the famed layout was even conceived, visitors to Monterey were enjoying the game. In the spring of 1897 the Del Monte Golf Course, a nine-hole track designed by Charles Maud, opened for play. Unlike most golf courses of the time, Del Monte was public, but because it was so closely linked with the luxe Hotel Del Monte, the course took on a greater cache than, say, New York's Van Cortland Park which was opened in 1895 as the first public golf course in the States.

As tourism and migration continued westward, they had a turbo-charging effect on the California economy. The Monterey Coast was a hot destination en route to a glorious future, but in the early 1900s, about a decade after the opening of the Del Monte course, the PIC almost botched the whole thing.

It was 1909, PIC was enjoying success with their lodging business and play was picking up at the Del Monte course.

That's when it was suggested by a local real estate firm, the Carmel Development Company, that a private seaside course be built as a further draw for PIC's lodging business. After some initial hesitation, the two parties agreed and CDC set out to create a private club comprised of 25 members, each of whom would pay $25 a year. That's right, the most beloved public golf course in the United States was nearly preempted by a private affair. By April of the following year PIC was actively promoting the project in flyers and other advertising. Destiny seemed to be restored when, over the course of the next few years, nearly half of the would-be members bailed on the project.

But Pebble's fate quickly took another dangerous turn. Following the failure of the private club scheme, PIC moved to Plan B: Simply sell the oceanfront land as residential lots. Amazingly enough, this course of action was actually pursued (albeit in lackadaisical fashion) until 1915, when Pebble's patron saint arrived.

In 1915 the Pacific Improvement Company hired a 30-year-old Yale graduate named Samuel F.B. Morse, a grandnephew of the inventor of Morse Code, to liquidate all of the company's land holdings. Eager to impress his new employers, Morse immediately sold off a single parcel of land overlooking majestic Stillwater Cove to a Mr. William Beatty. Morse perceptively commented at the time, "I will probably regret this." A year or so later, Morse came to his senses and changed course. The stocky New Englander who had moved to California upon graduation from college had an epiphany. Rather than filling in the coastline with roofs and walls, Morse felt that greater value could be generated by a shoreline public golf course. Fresh off the failure of the private club concept a few years prior, Morse's bosses at PIC were skeptical. Showing the skills that would one day make him the undisputed Prince of Pebble Beach, Morse sold them on his contention that by keeping the coastline clear of homes the value of the inland lots with ocean views would rise. Reason was further on Morse's side because the property boasted far more "view lots" than oceanfront lots.

Morse got the green light and promptly set to work on the project. Of course, there did remain the small problem of buying back any lots that had previously been sold. Morse was able to convince all but one owner—William H. Beatty—to sell their parcels back to PIC. Morse's and PIC's inability to buy back Beatty's land—Lot 3, Block 137—was reflected in the design of Pebble Beach when the awkward 5th hole was originally routed not toward the shore as originally hoped for, but inland and around the Beatty property. The dislocated hole would stick in the craw of course design purists for nearly a century. The "problem with the 5th" would not be resolved until the 1990s when the Beatty land was finally acquired and a new, more appropriate seaward 5th hole could be built.

With his vision largely intact and approvals in hand, Morse needed two more things: someone who could design the golf course and some publicity for it. The latter, he thought, might be gained by hosting a significant championship once the new course was completed. For years the California Golf Association had staged the California Amateur at nearby Del Monte, which had been expanded to 18 holes in 1912 by architect Herbert Fowler. Morse figured that if he could tempt the CGA on to his oceanside course, the project would likely be a success. While Morse's plan, followed by hundreds of course owners since, made perfect sense, his desire to host a meaningful championship at Pebble Beach would in time become a maddening obsession.

The time came for Morse to select an architect. There is strong evidence that he considered Charles Blair Macdonald for the job and may have even offered it to him. And there is lingering confusion as to whether he considered Donald Ross or Alister Mackenzie as well. As Morse wrote in his memoirs:

"There were two outstanding golf architects in those days—Charlie Macdonald, a wealthy man and first U.S. Amateur champion, and American; and Donald Ross in England. Mr. Macdonald couldn't be persuaded to do the job at Pebble Beach, and Donald Ross was in the English army ... "

As Hotelling suggests in his book on Pebble, it's likely that Morse simply confused Ross and Mackenzie when compiling his recollections. After all, this was 1916. Ross had left his native Scotland and moved to the United States in 1899. He was never in the English army. Mackenzie on the other hand, a native Brit, did serve two stints in the British army first in the Boer War and then in World War I, where he specialized in creating camouflage for the Royal Engineers. It was during this second tour of duty that Morse would most likely have been seeking Mackenzie's services.

What Morse lacked in specificity, he more than made up for with judgment. The three candidates mentioned—Macdonald, Ross and Mackenzie—were occupants of the top tier of the profession in 1916. By 1916 Macdonald's design portfolio included acknowledged gems such as Chicago Golf Club, St. Louis County Club, National Golf Links of America and Piping Rock Club on Long Island. For all his obstreperousness, his impact on a game that had only been played in the U.S. for a quarter-century was singular and echoes loudly today. Not only did he win the first (official) U.S. Amateur Championship, he was a founder of the USGA that sponsored it. The Walker Cup was Macdonald's idea. He's credited with coining the term "golf course architect." In fact, if one measured Macdonald's influence on the sport solely by the quality of his protégés he would be considered a giant. Seth Raynor, who would go on to a brilliant solo career, was a student and longtime partner of Macdonald's. A steadying influence on the bibulous Macdonald, Raynor had the primary design hand in virtually every course Macdonald "designed" from 1915 to 1925. This includes landmarks such as the Lido Golf Club (defunct), Mid Ocean, and the treacherous course at Yale.

Whereas Macdonald's broad and cranky influence on the game was felt in the areas of administration, competition, and golf course design, Donald Ross' focus was solely on the dirt. Although he did spend time as a club professional and he had studied the game under the legendary Old Tom Morris, Ross was a man of the earth. It was at Dornoch under the tutelage of the club's greenkeeper John Sutherland, that Ross found the seeds of his calling, a vocation described by Geoff Cornish and Ron Whitten in their book *The Architects of Golf* as "a lifelong interest in the propagation and maintenance of grass for golf and an understanding of the fundamentals of a good golf hole."

Ross's impact on golf course design is undeniable. Simply by being the profession's most prolific architect (he had a hand in the design or re-design of 413 courses) he was bound to make an impression on the art. Ross's courses were, for many American golfers of the early 20th century, an introduction to the game. This undoubtedly influenced the generation of designers who succeeded him and so on.

After moving to the United States in 1899 at the age of 27, the transplanted Scot worked briefly in Boston before being recruited by the Tufts family, which had made its fortune building soda fountains, to work winters at the resort they were developing in Pinehurst, North Carolina. His four ordinarily named courses at Pinehurst (christened simply No. 1, No. 2, No. 3, and No. 4) opened between 1901 and 1912. By the time No. 4 opened Ross was the most in-demand golf course designer in America, a position he would retain for nearly three decades until his death in 1948.

Ross was prolific and consistently excellent. Seminole, Timuquana, Plainfield, Pinehurst #2, Oakland Hills, Aronimink, Essex County Club, and Wannamoisett are just a few of the gems left behind by the master and his machine. Such is the wellspring of regard for Ross that over 100 U.S. national championships have been contested on his courses, more than any other architect.

Then there was Mackenzie, the Brit who, quite literally, wrote the book on golf course design. His book *Golf Architecture*, which is required reading for golf course design devotees, was published in 1920 and lays out Mackenzie's 13 "essential features" for quality golf course design. It is considered the blueprint for many of the golf courses in use today.

Born in Yorkshire, England, Mackenzie was a human force in the guise of a master golf course designer. After earning degrees in chemistry, natural science, and medicine from Cambridge, Mackenzie served as a surgeon in the Somerset Light Infantry in the Boer War. It was there, according to Cornish and Whitten, that Mackenzie "closely observed and analyzed the ability of Boer soldiers to hide effectively on treeless veldts."

Mackenzie veered into golf course design at the suggestion of the highly regarded British architect, Harry S. Colt. As the story goes, in 1907 Colt, a lawyer, spent an evening as a guest in Mackenzie's home. Colt, who was still practicing law and had designed only one golf course on his own Prenton Golf

Club (he had co-designed a new course for Rye Golf Club in 1894), saw models of greens and bunkers that Mackenzie had made as a hobby. He urged Mackenzie to join him in the design of nearby Alwoodley Golf Club. Mackenzie agreed, and within a few years he had left medicine and put out his design shingle. Although he never matched the output of Ross or the social standing of Macdonald, Mackenzie would become the game's first celebrity architect. In 1914 he staged a contest in *Country Life Magazine*. Readers were asked to submit a hole design with the promise that the winner, selected by a panel that included golf writer Bernard Darwin, noted player Horace Hutchinson, and architect Herbert Fowler, would have his hole included in Macdonald's final design of The Lido in New York.

Mackenzie's work on Cypress Point—an assignment awarded upon the death of the original designer and router of today's course, Seth Raynor—caught the attention of Bob Jones (Jones played Cypress during his trip to Pebble for the 1929 Amateur) and eventually earned Mackenzie the co-design role for Augusta National.

In the end, despite a Who's Who of early American golf course design staring him in the face, Morse made a mystifying selection. When it came to hiring a designer for his epic project, Morse opted for the head-scratching homespun combination of John C. "Jack" Neville and Douglas Grant. In the midst of what can be described as the Golden Age of American golf course architecture, Morse approached two locals who between them had never designed a single golf course in their lives.

Playing credentials they had. Both had won numerous state and local amateur titles. Neville, a real estate man, would earn a spot on the 1923 U.S. Walker Cup team. Grant, born in New York to a California mercantile family, had an impressive competitive resume as well. He won the 1908 Pacific Coast Championship before moving to England around 1910. He returned to California in 1916 and promptly finished runner-up in the 1916 Western Amateur and the 1917 and '18 California Ams. In late 1919 Grant, who spent most of his adult years in deafness due to a degenerative disease, returned to England with his family where he won many amateur titles and served as captain of the Royal St. George's Golf Club in Sandwich, England. Later in life—between his 50s and his 90s—Grant traveled quite often between England and California.

Clearly Neville, the lead designer, and Grant, who was to focus on bunkering, knew the game from a competitive standpoint, but their actual course design experience was nil. Of course, with gilded topography like that of the Monterey Coast, much of the work was already done. As Neville himself said in an interview with the *San Francisco Chronicle* in 1972, the canvas was largely complete. "God had already done a lot of the heavy lifting," he told the paper. "When it came to Pebble Beach Golf Links it was all there in plain sight. Very little clearing was necessary," he said. "The big thing, naturally, was to get as many holes as possible along the bay. It took a little imagination, but not much. Years before it was built, I could see this place as a golf links. Nature had intended it to be nothing else. All we did was cut away a few trees, install a few sprinklers, and sow a little seed."

By April 1916 the Neville/Grant layout for the 18 holes (awkward 5th hole included) had been completed. The designers had succeeded in "the big thing." It was time to build the course. In December of 1917, during construction of the Pebble Beach golf course, the Old Log Lodge, which had offered guests of the Hotel Del Monte a rustic alternative for meals and relaxation, burned down. This presented an opportunity to build a more comfortable structure that would twin nicely with the emerging links. But the PIC had had enough. They enlisted Morse to find a buyer for the property. The asking price: $1.3 million. After essentially sandbagging a bid from a New York syndicate, Morse moved to buy it himself. He teamed up with Herbert Fleishhacker, a San Francisco banker, to form Del Monte Properties Company, and on February 27, 1919 they acquired PIC's holdings for a total of $1,363,930.70 (After several subsequent ownership changes the property was acquired in 1999 by an investor group that included Clint Eastwood, Arnold Palmer, and Peter Ueberroth. The price: $820 million).

While the Morse-Fleishhacker purchase was certainly a deal, it did not come without headaches. For years, Pebble Beach mythology has maintained—and even its logo has attested to the fact—that the course opened in 1919. Not necessarily so. Pebble Beach actually hosted her inaugural rounds in a dismal two-day affair that spanned March 31 and, fittingly enough, April Fool's Day of 1918. Neville had invited some of the area's best players to take part in what was called the "christening" of the golf course—it would prove to be a baptism by fire and an unmitigated public relations disaster. When the contestants arrived they found the course's conditioning, which would be an issue for decades to come, embarrassing. The turf was spotty. Rocks routinely protruded the surface. The greens bore the hoof prints of sheep that still grazed the site. Criticism abounded about a handful of holes, and Neville was forced to backtrack. "The course is in an early state of development," he hemmed and hawed, "and it will be many months before all its fairways and greens are in condition for real tournament play."

The false start was a severe setback to Morse's grand plan to impress the CGA. The man who had paid $100,000 to build the golf course and who would soon pay $1.3 million for the entire property immediately shut down the new course and began scrambling for solutions. Interestingly enough, he turned to a local artist by the name of Francis McComas.

Recall that it was McComas who actually made the long mis-attributed remark about the "felicitous meeting of land and sea." McComas was an avid if not particularly gifted golfer, but he had a superb eye. He was born in Australia where he developed his interest in art. After a stint in Northern California, during which he studied at the Mark Hopkins Institute, and a period of further study in Paris, McComas returned to the United States in 1901 and emerged as an accomplished watercolorist, exhibiting often in California and across the country. In fact, according to "California Watercolors 1850-1970" by Gordon T. McClelland and Jay T. Last, McComas was one of only three California artists invited to exhibit at the famed 1913 New York Armory Show, a vastly influential exhibition recognized by historians as a landmark in the development of American art.

McComas was best known for his watercolors and the occasional oil on canvas or drawing, but for now, his medium was grass. He set to work on holes 1, 3, and 7, but his most notable tweak came on Pebble's uphill par-five 14th where he not only created the elegant two-tiered green that exists there today, but also inserted a frontal bunker to protect the upper left tier.

The McComas complex may be among the most visually satisfying at Pebble, but the acclaimed artist was putting lipstick on a pig. The fundamental weakness of Pebble Beach was its closing hole. In the eyes of the critics, among whom none mattered to Morse more than the CGA, the 18th hole at Pebble was still a nondescript, unexciting, graceless, stubby, and entirely forgettable par four.

After the opening-day debacle even Neville, who never charged a fee for his original design and was a pet of sorts to Morse, came under pressure. Morse ordered his designer back to work, and in a very rare instance of undermining Neville, ordered Hotel Del Monte manager, Carl Stanley, to take a more hands-on role in golf course management. Stanley quickly increased his course maintenance staff to 14 men, many of whom spent their days raking rocks from fairways. Stanley, attuned to complaints about hoof-marks on the putting surfaces, ordered a reduction in (and ultimately eviction of) the pesky sheep.

On February 22, 1919, nearly a year after the opening-day debacle, the revised golf course and the newly constructed lodge made their debuts. It was a society affair. The lead in the *San Francisco Examiner*'s coverage of the event read: "A fashionable gathering was present on Saturday night at the opening of Del Monte Lodge which promises in the future to be one of the favorite meeting places for society." Press reports focused on society matrons and their dresses, the light-hearted format and enjoyable atmosphere. In fact, the debut went well enough that the CGA finally agreed to hold the following year's (1920) California Amateur at Pebble Beach.

Although Morse had accomplished his goal of landing the state amateur on his new course it was an incomplete victory. The ever-fussy CGA brass left Pebble complaining again that the 18th hole was a "woefully poor finishing hole." Unless Morse could assuage the CGA's gripes, it was unlikely that the Championship would return in 1921, and Morse's plans to promote Pebble through meaningful tournaments would at least temporarily be dashed.

As stunning and beloved as the 18th hole is today, it's difficult to believe that it was once held in contempt, but the short (even by 1920s standards) 325-yarder, was Morse's enduring headache. Again, he cast about for solutions. One idea came from a wealthy local with the fitting name of Arthur "Bunker" Vincent. Vincent suggested to Morse that they fill in the rocks just behind the 17th green and build a new tee box that would not only add 35 yards to the 18th hole, but create a dramatic tee shot over water that allowed the player to bite off as much coastline as he could chew. Vincent's plan was enacted. The new hole now measured about 360 yards, and introduced to generations of heavy-breathing golfers the risk-reward excitement that comes with driving over Stillwater Cove. But while Vincent's addition undoubtedly made the hole better and provided one the great home-hole drives in the game, the balance of the 18th was still far from great. By now Morse knew the CGA. He knew that he would only win them over with bold and thoroughgoing change. The ultimate solution arrived courtesy of Pebble's growing nexus of golf and society.

In the 1920s, Pebble Beach, along with the broader Monterey Peninsula, was developing as a colony for social elites. The area was mentioned far more often in the society section than the sports pages. There was one woman who easily straddled both communities, a golf-loving and polo-playing New York society darling named Marion Hollins. Hollins' purchase of land at Pebble Beach is actually the first-ever mention of the community in the *New York Times*, which wrote in April of 1920 that the "metropolitan champion is expected to have purchased a piece of land at Pebble Beach near Del Monte, California, intending to erect a house and make her home there for part of the year." The story goes on to say that Hollins, who was preparing to sail for England to compete in the British Ladies championships, had recently played a few rounds at Pebble with a man named W. Herbert Fowler.

In 1920 British golf course architect William Herbert Fowler, who had spent much of the World War I era in the United States, was hired to remodel the Del Monte Course that he had lengthened eight years earlier. Given his relationship with Morse and his social standing in the community as evidenced by his friendship with Hollins, it could not have been a surprise when in 1921, Fowler was unloosed on Pebble's exasperating 18th hole.

Fowler, who had the credentials of a scratch player, acted boldly. He moved the par-four's green 170 yards up the coast to its current position, creating the dazzling waterfront 525-yard par-five that is still largely unchanged today. It would be an overstatement to say that Fowler's edit to the 18th secured Pebble Beach's place in golf history, but given the CGA's low regard for the old 18th hole, it's easy to assume that had Morse and Fowler not taken extreme measures, the CGA might never have again tapped Pebble as a championship venue. It follows that Pebble might not have caught wind as a serious golf mecca and that the old idea of selling ocean-front lots might have begun to look pretty promising to the course's new debt-laden owners.

CHAPTER 3

Newport of the West

IT WAS 1922. Pebble Beach was finally on the California golf map, but it was a far cry from the Pebble Beach that would go on to gain worldwide acclaim. Certainly it was more than good enough for an era in which golf courses were often hardscrabble un-artful affairs, but viewed in retrospect, via old photos and press clippings, the Pebble Beach of the early '20s looks downright shabby. Comparing the original Pebble with the course we know today is like comparing a Model T to a Lexus.

Golf writer and historian Geoff Shackelford speaks quite frankly of the early Pebble Beach. "If you look at the old photos of the era you get a clumsy, awful-looking golf course."

But the Pebble of the day was good enough for the CGA of the day, and it was gaining a reputation throughout the state as a serious test. Besides, it was the Roaring '20s, and Pebble Beach continued to be recognized as much for its high life and glamorous clientele as its golf. In 1923 Charles Chaplin and Pola Negri announced their engagement while visiting Pebble (the marriage would never take place.) Idols such as Charles Lindbergh, Howard Hughes, Salvador Dali— Morse referred to these people as "glitter and pomp"— branded Pebble Beach, its newly christened lodge and the Hotel Del Monte, as the "it place" to recreate in California.

Morse's joint was living up to its nickname as "the Newport of the West."

Morse himself used to tell a story about the casual, often liquid, nature of life and golf at Pebble Beach. It was 1915 and the drawn-out debate over Prohibition (which would be enacted in 1920) had begun. The issue permeated the air in social circles all over the country. The Cal Am final that year came down to Scotty Armstrong, a Hagenesque bon vivant, and Heine Schmidt, a teetotaler. Armstrong was a no-show for the tee time and was just about to be declared disqualified by the starter, when he showed up in his dinner jacket from the previous night. According to Morse, Armstrong yelled out, "Wait a few minutes," ran into the clubhouse where he took off his dinner jacket, put a belt around his dinner trousers, put on his golf shoes, rolled up his sleeves, knocked back a gin fizz and appeared on the first tee. After a hardy nine holes of competition, Armstrong hit the bar for a refill. After dispatching Schmidt for the title, Armstrong shook hands with Morse and said with a wide grin, "The wets win!"

However, for all its fun, restorative grace and social stature, Pebble's destiny was not hit-and-giggle golf, and Morse knew it. California was emerging as a hotbed of the game and the course—noted for its difficulty—was garnering attention throughout the west. News about Pebble Beach was even reverberating through the tweedy clubhouses of the northeast where the American game had taken root three decades earlier.

Morse, an easterner by birth, had gone through hair-pulling contortions to land the California Amateur, and now he set his sights on bigger game. Really big game: National championships. To get a sense of how impetuous a vision this was, consider that in 1920 California boasted a population of roughly 3.5 million people. According to the 1920 U.S. Census, this was less than 3 percent of the total U.S. population of 106 million. There were two million more people in New York City alone than in the whole of California. The Golden State was still considered a hardy frontier by many Americans. As David Fay, former executive director of the USGA reminds us, the early 20th century was a time of primitively constructed and unpaved roads, a time when, even for easterners "taking the Open to Shinnecock seemed like a trip." To Fay's point, a road map of Long Island from 1900 details two classes of roads, "good and fair."

But Morse had two resources to draw upon in his plan to land a national championship. The first was the increasingly popular Pebble Beach resort (even as late as the 1920s the Del Monte course remained as popular as Pebble Beach). The second was money. He put them both together and created the $5,000 Pebble Beach Open. No highbrow amateur action this time, instead Morse was going with star power. With the instincts of a fight promoter, Morse scheduled the tournament for a few days before the glitzy Los Angeles Open in order to attract the leading lights in the game. Names familiar even today showed up: Johnny Farrell, Al Watrous, Joe Turnesa, Bill Melhorn, Leo Diegel, Long Jim Barnes, Cyril Walker, and "Lighthorse" Harry Cooper.

In order to make certain that the tournament was covered precisely as he wanted it covered, the obsessively resourceful Morse actually launched a magazine called *Game and Gossip* and tapped a "writer" by the name of Earle Brown. Morse's goal of enshrining the event was exceeded to a fault by Brown, who all but drowned the facts of the event in his incomprehensibly syrupy coverage. To wit: "Names to be conjured with where golf has crept upon the mass. Rounds as sweet as the lilting melodies of the masters. Sublime, staggering, impossible shots fleshed to realities. ... Women's shrill voice sounding above the bass of men, pulling their favorite on, willing and willed. Spheres spurning clubheads to burn holes far down the green ... "

It went on like that ad nauseam, but buried in Brown's flowery conclusion was Morse's not-so-subtle pitch for the future: "Pebble Beach was a worthy playground and if made an annual one needs but announcement for everyone's return and those who will harken to their praises. We have had our first stellar championship with the majority of Kings competing. We shall have them all in the future."

What Brown lacked in brevity he made up for in prescience. The kings would, in fact, come to Pebble, but not before a little internal housekeeping. In the wake of that inaugural Pebble Beach Open (won by Cooper), most of the players' comments about the course, particularly those about the refashioned 18th hole, were glowing. But there seemed to be a glowering consensus about the 8th hole. It is today one of the great holes in all of golf, requiring intelligence on the drive and bravery on the second shot, which must carry a roiling saltwater chasm before homing in on a small green perched precipitously on a ledge above the water. Herbert Warren Wind once described the hole: "You trudge up the slope, after your blind tee shot, and, suddenly, spread before you is what may well be the most dramatic par-four in all the world."

The complaint in 1926 was not with the drive or the knee-knocking second-shot, but with the ill-suitedness of the green complex to accept a long-iron shot. The complex had originally been designed by Neville and Grant, but had been retouched by Alister Mackenzie in advance of Morse's Pebble Beach Open. How Mackenzie got his paws on one of the great course's greatest holes is a tribute to both his timing and his indefatigability.

What happened was that on January 23, 1926, at the age of 51, Seth Raynor died in a Palm Beach hotel. The cause was pneumonia, no doubt brought on by a feverish cross-continental work schedule that had the in-demand course architect traveling between Hawaii and Florida. Raynor's untimely death meant that Marion Hollins, who had hired him to design both Monterey Peninsula and Cypress Point, needed someone to finish those jobs. Unlike Morse who settled for local design talent in creating Pebble Beach, Hollins went A-list. She recruited Alister Mackenzie, who quickly agreed to take the job, and who moved to (and fell in love with) California. Working only a short distance from Pebble Beach, Mackenzie now had ample opportunity to play Pebble and speak with Morse and his influencers about the course's flaws. One can assume he was less than bashful.

Mackenzie, in what some have described as a possible "audition" for future re-design work (work that never came) re-did the bunkering at Pebble's 8th and 13th greens. The problem was that prior to final completion of the re-bunkering, Mackenzie was called to a design job in Australia (Royal Melbourne) and so the 8th hole green complex that was played in Morse's so-called Pebble Beach Open was only a stop-gap, but its unfinished appearance was the focus of complaints. When Mackenzie returned from Australia in 1927, he completed the work to the plaudits of current and future critics.

By 1927 the USGA had staged 31 U.S. Amateur Championships. With 11 of those championships having been contested in the New York area, five in Pennsylvania and four in New England, the U.S. Amateur had largely been a northeastern affair. Thanks to Charles Blair Macdonald the Amateur did make seven stops in Illinois between 1897 and 1923, and it made occasional trips to places such as Cleveland, Ohio, and Grosse Pointe Farms, Michigan, but by 1927 the Havemeyer Trophy had never traveled west of Minneapolis, Minnesota. So, the USGA's announcement in1927 that the U.S. Amateur was coming to Pebble Beach was a landmark in golf history. It mirrored both the demographic arc of an era and the life of Roger Dearborn Lapham, the USGA insider who brought the Amateur westward.

CHAPTER 4

The Diamond Polishers

ROGER DEARBORN LAPHAM was a New Yorker by birth, but a Californian by inclination. With five uncles on his mother's side having been avid seamen, Lapham was born with a wistful fondness for the bounding main. From the moment his uncle, George Dearborn, founder of the American-Hawaii Steamship Company, invited the 17-year-old Lapham to enjoy a company steamship ride to Hawaii in 1900, Lapham was hooked. He would complete his education at Harvard and move west to San Francisco, eventually becoming, in 1925, president of A-H upon the death of his uncle.

Lapham's career took a turn for the political when in the years following the 1934 general strike by the city's longshoremen, he took on Harry Bridges, boss of the West Coast longshoremen, in a debate. Lapham represented management and Bridges the union. The topic: whether or not the union should be running its own hiring halls.

According to a *Time* magazine article from July 1946 (the ebullient Lapham was featured on the cover), the combatants "met in a hall packed with Bridges men. The longshoremen hooted at the red-faced, white-haired capitalist and ship owner. Lapham put his feet apart and shouted back. Bridges' longshoremen ended the night by applauding Lapham for his frankness and sportsmanship. "That day," the magazine wrote, "Roger Lapham walked onto the political stage."

Lapham would remain an enlightened effusive force at the intersection of San Francisco business and politics. In fact, the jowly middle-handicapper described as a "zestful extrovert" would ultimately be elected mayor in 1944.

Lapham was a showman with a CEO's focus, and he loved to dance. In 1945, his second year as mayor, Lapham, a Republican, toured Northern California. In one small town he joined in a roadhouse dance with railroad workers and their wives. He stopped at another small Indian town, Yreka, and cut the rug with the natives until 4 a.m. When he took time for a cooling skinny-dip in the Trinity River, an Indian squaw and children stopped to stare. Hizzoner was unfazed: "If that squaw hasn't anything better to do than watch an old fool like me in swimming, why, to hell with it—let her look," Time reported.

While in San Francisco political circles Lapham is remembered for his success in labor relations; for his reluctance to proclaim a day of prayer in San Francisco (on the grounds that "any San Franciscan who wanted to pray was at liberty to do so, any time"), and for his famed yet failed plan to rid the city of its beloved cable cars. Golf historians see him as the first president of Cypress Point and credit him with steering that club through the Depression. (At one point in those lean years the club's roster dwindled to fewer than 50 members). Secondly, it was Lapham, the socially wired Ivy-leaguer with connections on both coasts, who through his role as a vice president and executive committee member of the USGA, and his familiarity with Monterey Coast golf, likely brought the 1929 national amateur championship west.

But precisely because this was the coming out party for

Chris Millard

California golf, there was a lot of work to do. The course needed an overhaul. Furthermore, disputes on equipment and the properties of the golf ball were already prevalent in the late 1920s. Herbert Jacques was the chairman of what the USGA then called the Committee on Implements and the Ball. During a January 1928 USGA meeting he reported the progress his committee was making on ball-testing, telling attendees about a machine they were working on which would measure the resiliency of golf balls. He said, "dependable data in measuring the resiliency of golf balls are now assured." He went on to suggest that the machine would enable the USGA to "control driving power" without having to mess with a ball's size or weight.

The early criticisms of Pebble from the CGA—combined with the bubbling equipment controversy and the preparation of Pebble for its national debut—was going to require some deft handiwork. The USGA, which would not take a true hands-on role in championship course preparations until the mid-1950s, left it to Lapham to work with Del Monte Properties to modernize Pebble Beach. Lapham's hand-picked architectural advisors were the odd couple of Robert W. Hunter and H. Chandler Egan. Hunter, an avowed socialist (in 1910 he ran for governor of Connecticut on the Socialist ticket), was one of the world's leading authorities on sociology. He also happened to love golf, a sport whose Scottish roots were certainly populist but whose American interpretation had grown increasingly elitist. Somehow, the Indiana-born Hunter, who had written serious and searching tomes such as *Poverty*, *Labor in Politics* (imagine the discussions he had with Lapham), *Why We Fail As Christians*, and *Revolution*, had been able to bridge the yawning social chasm between his politics and his passion. In fact, in 1926

Hunter, one of the game's early counter-cultural devotees—the original Shivas Irons—would write another book, *The Links*, which remains one of the finest and most influential books ever printed on the topic of golf course architecture.

Egan was more representative of 1920s golf. The handsome son of Highland Park (north of Chicago) had played his youth golf at Exmoor County Club. He became one of American golf's earliest amateur stars by capturing the 1902 NCAA Championship while enrolled at Harvard. He would go on to win a team gold and an individual silver in the 1904 Olympic Games, as well as the U.S. Amateur title in 1904 and 1905, and the Western Am in 1902, 1904, 1905, and 1907. In 1911 at the age of 27, Egan, who had been seduced by tales of fortunes being made in the Pacific Northwest's apple-growing industry, moved to Oregon: 300 miles from the nearest golf course. The move, while curious to many observers at the time, would eventually produce tangible benefits for American golfers. He began dabbling in design work almost immediately upon arrival in Oregon, designing Rogue Valley Country Club in 1911, and collaborating with George Junor on Tualatin Country Club in 1912. Over the next two decades, fueled not only by his preparation of Pebble Beach for the 1929 Amateur, but by the roughly two dozen courses he would go on to design in the Northwest, Egan blossomed into one of the game's premier player-architects, a remarkably successful and durable dual calling that would last until his death in 1936. He won the 1915 Northwest Pacific Championship, and would do so again in 1920, '23, '25, and '32. He would play on the 1930 and 1934 Walker Cup teams at the respective ages of 46 and 50. Ironically, Egan's greatest stand would occur in 1929 on Pebble Beach, the course he had now been asked to stiffen.

The goals of the Pebble Beach preparation project, as stated in detail by Egan, were simple: First, Egan and Hunter were desirous of making a minimum of radical changes, but where changes were needed, the team had come to two conclusions: "The first nine needed stiffening and if possible greater length" (as evidenced earlier by Herbert Jacques, equipment was already an issue), and 16 of the 18 greens needed "returfing, reshaping, and retrapping." As Egan wrote: "Some of the old greens were rather old-fashioned, unattractive, and dull, some were a bit unfair in their slope and lack of visibility, and almost none of them offered a real target for an iron shot."

Egan set the bar extremely high—narrow fairways; deep, moist rough, and frighteningly fast greens—and the USGA never looked back. In fact, some have argued that Egan's set-up for Pebble Beach became the de facto model for future USGA set-ups.

This may be a good time to point out that even though Mackenzie was not selected for either the Pebble Beach original design or the U.S. Amateur prep job, he was not without influence over the course. As discussed, he did make some changes in advance of Morse's Pebble Beach Open, but it's likely that Mackenzie's input was much broader, if once removed. There was a formal business partnership among Egan, Mackenzie, and Hunter. In fact, it was Hunter who urged both Mackenzie and his brother, C.A., to California, leading Alister to land the design job at Cypress Point and getting Charles some re-design work at both Pebble and Monterey Peninsula. Mackenzie had already designed Cypress and Monterey Peninsula (both with Hunter), and Mackenzie had used his brother's construction company to build them.

Alister Mackenzie was not an overly pleasant man, and

Joe Mayo, the head superintendent at Pebble, didn't like him (or C.A. for that matter). Mayo is believed to have persuaded his boss, Samuel Morse, to keep both Mackenzies at arm's length. But given the professional closeness among Egan, Hunter, and Mackenzie, many historians believe that whatever input Egan or Hunter had on Pebble Beach actually reflected Mackenzie's thinking.

The hallmark of the Egan-Hunter (-Mackenzie) preparation of Pebble Beach for the 1929 Amateur was undoubtedly the re-bunkering. The greens were in many cases, completely surrounded by wild, visually striking "imitation dunes" that featured un-manicured edging and were interspersed with sand and grass like a windward beach. According to Egan, the look was the brainchild of his and superintendent Mayo's, neither of whom, Egan wrote, had ever "seen this type of bunkering done before but we had faith in the idea and after a few experiments achieved a result that we hope will continue to be as good as it seems at this writing."

Although the dunes accomplished their mission of refreshing the look and stiffening the challenge of Pebble Beach for the 1929 Amateur, they wouldn't last. They were hell to manage. With no lips or capes to block the Pacific winds— particularly winter gales—it became virtually impossible to keep them stocked with sand.

"The dunes-y natural look didn't keep because it was too expensive to maintain," said golf course historian, writer, and architect, Geoff Shackelford, who points out that around this time Cypress Point filled in 35 bunkers because even it couldn't afford the upkeep. "If Cypress was struggling, you can be sure Pebble was, too" Shackelford added.

Over the intervening 80 years, the humps and hollows created by Egan have been grassed over, however remnants of the old dunes-y look are still visible. Most notably they can be seen among the rough mounds surrounding the 17th green, awaiting stray tee shots, hoping for their chance to make history.

But in 1929, with his elegant if ill-fated bunkers crowning a course that was now playing by his estimate "a stroke or two" more difficult, Pebble Beach was now indisputably an H. Chandler Egan design. Credit for the famed figure-8 routing still belongs to Neville (and Grant), but Egan's changes were transformative.

"Egan re-did the golf course," says Shackelford. "It's Neville's routing, but it's Egan's golf course. He doesn't get the credit he deserves but it's his."

One reason that Neville (and Grant) remained front and center is that that's precisely where Morse wanted him. Neville was popular and he was local. He made for great copy. As a local boy made good he was a marketable commodity. Neville also had the ability to make Morse's life miserable. Not only was he a real estate salesman who brokered sales of many Pebble Beach-area properties, he also oversaw *Pacific Golf and Motor Magazine*, an influential publication among the western travel and leisure set. Throughout his career, Morse was protective of Neville's—not to mention his course's—image and he wasn't about to let facts muddy up a good story. In fact, in a 1973 magazine article by Anne Germain entitled "Pebble Beach: The Way It Was," the writer makes the point that the golf course is recognized as among the best in the world and reinforces her statement with a bold-faced lie from Morse: "We didn't let anybody monkey around with it."

As 1929 and the U.S. Amateur approached, word had been making its way around golf circles that the California course, largely unknown to Eastern players, was being prepped to the gills. One New York sportswriter struck a tone of foreboding when he wrote: "H. Chandler Egan ... is rebuilding the Pebble Beach course at Monterey for the U.S. Amateur Championship ... (Tommy) Armour, (Bobby) Cruickshank and others who have been prospecting for golf gold in California during the past winter declare that Eastern amateurs will have their eyes opened when they see what the coast has to offer ..."

The 1929 field sparkled. It boasted eight former U.S. Amateur champions including prohibitive favorite and defending champion, Bob Jones. The 26-year-old Georgian had already won the Amateur in 1924,' '25, '27 and '28 (He had also finished runner-up to George von Elm in 1926 and would, of course, go on to win in 1930 at Merion to complete his historic Grand Slam). If anyone could afford to feel comfortable as the Amateur approached, it was Jones, but that wasn't his style. Jones was a worrywart who dealt with stress-related illnesses for much of his life. So when Jones' mouthpiece and friend, O.B. Keeler, sent a telegram to the USGA's Lapham four months prior to the Championship, informing him that Jones intended to reach California a full month in advance of play "in order to become thoroughly acquainted with the Pebble Beach course," it was not only an indication of Jones' good manners, but of his intensity.

Even though *Golfer's Magazine* pinned Jones as the favorite—"the National Amateur simmers down to Bobby Jones against the field"—there were other notable and realistic contenders, chief among them Lawson Little, who had already won the first of his two Northern California Amateur titles and would, in a few more years, make history by winning both the U.S. Amateur and British Amateur in both 1934 and 1935. Another contender was Charlie Seaver (father of future Baseball Hall of Fame pitcher Tom Seaver), who would become a fixture in California amateur golf circles.

After an August 27 practice round (his first-ever round at Pebble) and after several rounds at other local golf courses, Jones declared Pebble Beach a "true test," but admitted that he did expect to see 70 broken on the par-72 course. After two practice rounds of 73-73, the media could be forgiven for thinking that if Jones couldn't break par maybe no one could. Two days later Jones shot a two-under 70. The next day he took on Cypress Point (Jones would actually go fishing the day before the medal rounds commenced).

Prohibitive favorite Jones (who was paired with Jack Neville for the two medal rounds) tied for medalist honors with rounds of 70-75, and tied with Eugene Homans who shot 72-73. In a preview of the Championship, respected golf writer William D. Richardson of the *New York Times* pinpointed the treachery lurking in Pebble's closing holes, describing the 17th and 18th "as two of the most terrifying holes on the entire layout." Richardson's eye would prove prescient, as both holes played decisive roles not only in that championship but in others to come.

The 17th had made its presence known to Jones early on. In the first qualifying round, Jones had pushed his tee shot to the right. The ball appeared to be heading for the water when it struck a spectator on the back and ricocheted on to the edge of the green. Jones was fortunate to get up and down for par.

In his first round of match play, Jones took on Johnny Goodman, an Omaha caddie who famously took a job on a cattle car in order to pay his freight to California (a few months earlier he had done the same to travel to Winged

Foot for the Open). Few gave Goodman a chance, but as the Nebraskan and the Georgian headed to the tape, Jones, who had not led at all in the match, remained 1-down. The Atlantan had a chance to close the gap with a 10-foot birdie putt at 17, but he rimmed the cup. Goodman stood dormie and went on to win the match on the 18th hole (this despite the fact that Jones carded a 75 to Goodman's 76).

Goodman's win (or, more accurately, Jones' loss) still ranks as one of the great upsets in the game; a little-known train-jumper from Omaha turns back the game's greatest icon. The crowd, so large that for the first time organizers were forced to use soldiers rather than the usual Boy Scouts as marshals, was stunned. As one scribe put it: "Five thousand people walked away as from the scene of a particularly atrocious murder."

While Jones' victories in the U.S. Open gave that championship greater status, his first-round loss to Goodman did the same for the U.S. Amateur. The thinking went that if Pebble Beach and the U.S. Amateur were too tough for the invincible Jones, they had to be superb. Hence, Pebble and the 1929 Amateur became more than geographic landmarks in the westward migration of the game, they became benchmarks in the evolution of the sport. Pebble had earned its stripes, not as the place where a guy named Harrison Johnston eventually won, but as the place where the great Jones lost.

CHAPTER 5

Of Crashes, Clashes, and Bashes

THE 1929 U.S. AMATEUR was completed on September 7, 1929. Just 52 days later, the bottom fell out of the United States economy. Like every other facet of American life, golf ground to a heart-rending halt.

During the resulting Great Depression, the Wealth Belt that spanned from Northern California's mining fortunes to L.A.'s flamboyant movie scene, snapped. Pebble was beached. In fact, during the Depression the only profitable arm of Morse's Del Monte empire was said to have been a sand plant located on what is now The Links at Spanish Bay. If the Depression was rocking Morse's empire one can be sure it was hammering the rank and file. In Jerry Stewart's book about the course's colorful caddies, entitled *Pebble Beach: Golf and the Forgotten Men*, the point is made by one long-time caddie that "back then guys lived day-to-day. If they didn't make a loop they didn't have dinner." One Pebble caddie at the time, Dyer Wilson Jr., actually spent 90 days in jail for stealing goats in nearby Ojai. The goats were owned by an Ojai judge.

The Depression was like a heavy wet blanket thrown over the giddiness of the day. No one was immune from its pall. The well-off were reduced to savers, the middle class to scavengers, and the poor to denizens of the soup line. As the science fiction writer Isaac Asimov, who turned nine years old in 1929, once said, "No one can possibly have lived through the Great Depression without being scarred by it."

While many of his friends in finance and business were forced to sell, Morse, who had already shown flashes of sharp-wittedness and good timing, did the opposite. He doubled down. The swoon in the U.S. banking industry put pressure on Morse's partner, banker Herbert Fleishhacker, to liquidate his holdings in Del Monte Properties. In an amicable deal, Morse acquired the vast bulk of Fleishhacker's stock, leaving Fleishhacker with only a small number of shares but a seat in the board.

Local real estate sales screeched to a halt. In fact, according to Neal Hotelling's book, Morse intentionally halted sales rather than compete with distressed local sellers who were selling their homes for desperately low asking prices.

The facilities at Pebble Beach remained open for business, but Morse shifted from serving the financially crippled elite of the day to investing in the upper crust of the future. He focused on attracting to Carmel Bay young, active collegians, the people who would be the deep-pocketed bankers and film producers of the next decade. Ever aware of the power of the moving image, Morse also regularly welcomed Hollywood productions to his scenic seaside location.

But Del Monte Properties was running in the red and loss was all around. For instance, Cypress Point was near default on $150,000 owed to Morse, but Morse forgave the note and saved the club. Still, neither Morse nor Del Monte Properties could operate like this forever. By 1935, Morse, like everyone else in America, was feeling financial pressure. In search of a cash infusion, he sold off the water works that supplied fresh water to much of Monterey County from an artesian well system beneath his property (along with the sale, Morse shrewdly negotiated a 50-year price freeze on his company's water bill). He used some of the proceeds from that sale to acquire from descendants of the Jacks family an additional 1,400 acres (including the old Del Monte Golf Course) on which he built low-to middle-end housing for local fishery workers.

The 1930s were a lost decade for many, including Pebble Beach, which had been reduced to a shadow of its bon vivant self. But through Morse's deft helmsmanship, the course, The Lodge, and the parent company stayed intact and were able to christen the early 1940s with a USGA twin bill. The 1940 U.S. Women's Amateur, won by Betty Jameson, was played at Pebble Beach, and plans were also in place for the course to host the 1942 U.S. Am. Those plans, like so many in the early 1940s were scrapped by the advent of World War II (no USGA championships were staged between 1942 and 1945).

The cancellations reflected not only the fact that millions of Americans had enlisted in the war effort, they also underscored a shift in American sensibilities and priorities. Golf, always considered a luxury, was now seen as a truly needless extravagance. Even for those few golfers who still had both the money to play and the spine to risk the critics' ire, both courses and equipment had grown scarce. As players bolted the game, private clubs folded, and as the nation's resources—particularly steel and rubber—were marshaled for the war effort, shafts, clubheads and balls grew scarce. In his book, *When War Played Through: Golf During World War II*, John Strege, points to a January 4, 1942 article in The *New York Times* that said, "While production of a few (rubber) products considered essential for civilian and industrial use will continue, golf and tennis balls, bathing apparel, toy balloons, and similar items will be virtually eliminated."

Like golf, other extravagances, whether a trip to the shore or a stay at a luxury hotel, were few and far between. For people like Morse, who had made a living helping other people live it up, the war years presented real problems. But Morse, ever the problem-solving dealmaker, had an idea: With more and more military personnel—particularly Navy flyers—needing to gather in California for training, perhaps they needed a place to stay. Morse persuaded the Navy to lease the Del Monte Hotel for $33,000 a month.

Morse's Pebble survived the War, so much so that in the immediate wake of V-J Day, the course was awarded the 1947 U.S. Amateur (won by Skee Riegel) and the '48 Women's Amateur (featuring Morse's daughter, Mary in the field), won by Grace Lenczyk. The renewal of competitive golf in America signaled that levity and leisure were on the rebound. It was in this happy moment that the game's most beloved golf tournament found new life.

It was formally known as the Bing Crosby Professional-Amateur, but it will forever be remembered as "The Crosby." The first iteration, The Crosby Clambake was played in 1937 at Rancho Santa Fe County Club, near San Diego County's Del Mar Race Track. Ironically, the tournament that became famous for its duffery was founded by a very good player—Crosby played in the 1950 British Amateur at St. Andrews. The initial idea was to bring together low-handicappers from Lakeside Golf Club in Los Angeles, where Der Bingle was a member, with a few dozen touring professionals as the latter passed through the West Coast swing of the PGA schedule.

That first event was won by a 24-year-old Sam Snead

who, after being presented a check for $500 by Crosby himself, turned to the host and said, "If it's all the same to you Bing, I'd rather have the cash."

The alchemic interaction of men, golf, sports, Hollywood, and booze altered the trajectory of the event. Almost from day one, The Crosby became known less for the seriousness of its competition than for the severity of its hangovers. But the original Crosby Clambake (so named despite the fact that there never was a clambake; in fact, the original fare was barbecue prepared under a pepper tree grove on the crooner's nearby ranch) was short-lived.

The War Years quieted the party from 1943 until 1946, but as peace took root, Morse and the civic leaders of Northern California were eager to capitalize on the pre-war publicity that Pebble Beach had earned as a golf destination. They approached Crosby about the possibility of reviving his frat party at Pebble. Included in their pitch: tournament rounds at two of the finest private tracks in the area, Monterey Peninsula Country Club and Cypress Point. Crosby's agreement and the resulting decades of Pebble Beach pars, parties, and publicity would secure Pebble's place in the national golfing consciousness as a destination for first-class golf and gaiety. If you have any doubts about what Crosby's relocation meant to the local community, consider that in 1947, the first year the Clambake was staged at Pebble, the city of Monterey made him an honorary police chief.

For the next few decades the party raged on. Crosby's connections in law enforcement likely buffered the host and his elite invitees from pesky local ordinances. Consider the 1951 bash. In his foreword to *The Crosby: The Greatest Show in Golf*, the late Dwayne Netland's 1975 book about the tournament, Crosby tells the story of attending the traditional blow-out at Francis Brown's nearby mansion with his own 13-year-old son, Lindsay in tow. While Lindsay puttered around the estate with the gardener, Crosby fully partook of the evening's refreshments. Bing eventually left the party at about 4 a.m. As hard as it is to believe in this day and age, Crosby drove home, with Lindsay in the front and a few wobbly buddies in the back. The next morning, none other than Bob Hope approached young Lindsay with an avuncular concern and asked the youngster how he got home the previous night. Lindsay explained that his father had driven the group home without incident. When an incredulous Hope asked how the group could have let the over-served Crosby drive, Lindsay responded, "He was the best we had."

The tourney was secondary. It became a fashionable excuse for a golf-loving swath of sports heroes, Hollywood stars, business moguls and the glitterati of Northern California to gather in the corduroy and cashmere climes of Carmel each February. Such was the social buzz around The Crosby that until her death in 1999, the *San Francisco Chronicle*'s Pat Steger, covered the event, not in the sports section, but in the paper's society pages.

In those early Crosby years Pebble began to operate on three parallel tracks. Year-round it remained a well-worn public facility, providing some of the most beautiful golf vistas in the game to paying hackers of any stripe. In winter it devolved into the sodden playground of Bing's buddies, and in the odd summer it managed to maintain its place among the great championship tests by hosting significant tourneys, none of them more foretelling than the 1961 U.S. Amateur at Pebble Beach.

Beefy 21-year-old Jack Nicklaus had won the Amateur in 1959 at the Broadmoor in Colorado, but his defense in 1960 at St. Louis Country Club had been abysmal: after winning two matches, the second against his boisterous pal Phil Rodgers, Nicklaus lost focus. Six three-putts (one from gimme range) in his third-round match against Arkansan Charlie Lewis sent the defending champion back to Columbus.

He came to Pebble in September 1961 inspired by the beauty and the test that awaited him ("I fell in love with Pebble Beach from the moment I first played it in practice that year," he said), and motivated by the memory of his early exit in St. Louis. He was a force. Accompanied by local caddie Al "Dede" Gonsalves (the same man who looped Harrison Johnston to victory in the 1929 Am), Nicklaus stormed the field. Not a single one of his matches reached the 18th hole. That week Nicklaus not only found love at the beach, he found the true depth of his skills. "I simply played the finest golf of my life up to that point," he said.

Notably, it was at Pebble Beach during practice rounds for the 1961 U.S. Amateur that Nicklaus, with the encouragement of his friend and future PGA Tour commissioner, Deane Beman, first began "walking off" the yardages of a golf course. He used his self-compiled yardage book throughout the trip and played every round under par. In fact, Nicklaus still has that same cheat sheet. "I've refurbished it a couple of times," he said. "It may not be the exact same piece of paper, but I have the same yardages, and the same book, and probably about half the trees and markers that I had are gone."

By late in the decade, Pebble Beach, like the country itself, was undergoing cultural change. In 1969 Samuel F.B. Morse, who quite rightfully became known as "the Duke of Del Monte" died at the age of 83. While his widow would retain control of the property for many years, other changes—good and bad—were in the offing.

Also in the late 1960s, Mr. San Francisco-area Golf (and future president of the USGA), Sandy Tatum was asked to restore the nearly half-a-century old course. The ostensible mission was to restore a layout that had fallen into disrepair, job enough given the stature that the course enjoyed, but, said Tatum, the assignment carried much broader implicit responsibilities. "Basically, we were restoring it," he said in an unpublished oral history on file at the USGA Archives. "But it also held with it the possibility of Pebble Beach one day holding an Open Championship."

Tatum, a very successful lawyer by trade but a golf purist and historian at heart, almost predictably sought out Jack Neville, the course's original co-designer and found him living in obscurity in nearby Pacific Grove. Their subsequent collaboration is described by Tatum as one of the most satisfying experiences of his life. Working with "Jack gave me two things I needed for the project," said Tatum in an interview with the website GolfClubAtlas.com. "It gave me his perceptions even though it was my project, and it gave me the credibility I needed to do what I thought should be done."

Tatum's take on Neville's original work at Pebble Beach is that "he did the best possible routing of that piece of earth, and I was thrilled to be involved with him. He was also thrilled to be working again on the course he created." The duo made strategic changes to roughly half of Pebble Beach's 18 holes, including adding a new greenside bunker on the 1st hole and new longer tees on Holes 2 and 3. They added bunkers to the left side of the 9th hole to stop players from running up the un-irrigated hardpan then found there. They lengthened the 10th hole and re-bunkered the landing area. They also added a penal bunker on the right of the landing area of the par-four 16th hole. (The bunker would go on to garner more than its share of attention in the closing stages of the 1982 Open.)

By the late 1960s, with four USGA championships and nearly two decades of Crosby-inspired publicity, Pebble had emerged as the best-known and most beloved golf course west of the Mississippi, yet the course that had also hosted a spate of prestigious state Opens and Ams had never hosted the big Kahuna, the U.S. Open. Why?

The answer is a combination of location and money. Pebble is about 120 miles south of the nearest major city, San Francisco. That posed a real problem for Open organizers who were used to attracting fans from massive population centers such as New York, Detroit, San Francisco, Philadelphia, St. Louis, and Boston.

"The U.S. Open had never gone to a course that was so far removed from a commercial center, a metropolitan center," Tatum once said.

Granted, the previous USGA Championships, most recently the 1961 Amateur, were critical successes, but U.S. Amateur organizers don't expect a crowd, U.S. Open organizers do. There was an enduring question among USGA brass and local golf officials: What if you staged an Open and no one came? Stunning as it sounds today, prior to 1972 organizers never took the Open to Pebble Beach because they feared that no one else would make the trip. Secondly, since Pebble was a public course it lacked the ready-made volunteer base that private host clubs offer. The question loomed: what would organizers do for volunteers? This, of course, was an issue as early as 1929, when the USGA had to use local military personnel, members from nearby private clubs, and even the Boy Scouts to help run the tournament.

The final issue was conditioning. With heavy public play and limited budgets for maintenance, conditions at Pebble

Beach had long been an issue. Combine those concerns and the USGA was understandably anxious about hosting its most revered championship at Pebble.

"We thought going to Pebble was risky," said the late Frank Hannigan, who joined the USGA in 1961 and would serve as executive director from 1983 to 1988. "We had no clue if anyone would go down there in 1972. We even put in the contract that we would get $100,000 no matter what in terms of admissions income."

But with the renovation by Tatum and Neville, the course was deemed worth the risk. Contestants found a new Pebble Beach, far tougher, and with the USGA's tending, far meaner than the Pebble they had seen in umpteen Crosbys or the most recent U.S. Amateur. As Nicklaus wrote in his autobiography, "Pebble Beach was tough enough for most of us just the way Jack Neville and Donald (sic) Grant built it, but when those small, sharply contoured greens got some USGA ordered rolling and triple cutting before the final round, then high winds evaporated every drop of moisture out of them, it turned into Godzilla." In fact, at one point during the '72 Open Nicklaus turned to then USGA executive director P.J. Boatwright Jr. and said, "What did you do with all the grass?"

The set-up for that '72 Open was nothing short of brutal. Billy Casper, who had already won two U.S. Opens at torture chambers such as Winged Foot (1959) and Olympic (1966) pointed to Pebble as a singular challenge. "It was the first time you had to absolutely plan the perfect shot, shot after shot, then execute the perfect shot, then be lucky," he said.

Nicklaus was paired in the final round with Lee Trevino, who had defeated the Golden Bear in a playoff at Merion in the preceding year's U.S. Open. Entering the final stanza with a one-shot lead over the likes of Trevino, Arnold Palmer,

Johnny Miller, and Bruce Crampton, Nicklaus carded an unusually high final-round 74 that included a double bogey on 10 after an errant drive onto the beach. But Sunday's stiff winds kept his challengers at bay, and with the help of his superhuman 1-iron on—of all holes—the 17th, Nicklaus prevailed by three over Bruce Crampton.

His history of good play and good fortune at Pebble Beach instilled in Nicklaus a lasting respect and affection for the seaside treasure. Since 1972 he has been quoted dozens of times saying that, "If I had one round of golf left to play it would be at Pebble Beach."

The course, which stumbled at its baptism, had graduated to the acme of major championship tests. In five years' time it would host the PGA Championship, but off course things were not progressing as smoothly. The Pebble Beach Corporation was listed on the American Stock Exchange on March 30, 1977. This allowed a company known as Deltec to accumulate a large chunk of PBC stock through its own subsidiary companies, and ultimately take control of Pebble Beach. Later on, after Deltec's liquidation, its chairman A. Thomas Taylor, along with his auto-scion partner Henry Ford II, took ownership of Pebble Beach. In 1979 the property was sold to Twentieth Century Fox, which two years earlier had released Star Wars, the most profitable movie ever made. The seaside locale for which the late Sam Morse spent $1.3 million some 60 years earlier sold to the flush Hollywood studio for $81.5 million.

The successive changes in ownership indicate that while a long-term investment in the incomparable seaside property was a sure thing, the operating profit of the resort was skimpy. Several people who were close to the property in that era confirm the resort's financial difficulties. Terry Jastrow, who would become well known in golf circles as the director of hundreds of golf tournaments on ABC Sports, including the dramatic 1982 U.S. Open telecast, shares some insight into Pebble's struggles. In the Late 1960s and early 1970s, Jastrow was a production assistant with the network. Among his many grunt-work responsibilities was making on-site reservations for all of the network's announcers and brass. When the ABC team came to Pebble either for a Crosby or a USGA Championship, Jastrow would deal with Pebble's then reservation manager Tom Oliver.

Over the years, as Jastrow moved up the line at ABC, Oliver rose the ranks at Pebble, eventually becoming general manager of the resort. About two months prior to the 1982 Open, Oliver called Jastrow and suggested that the next time Jastrow was in the area for a site survey, the two share dinner. At the well-known Rocky Point restaurant, Oliver poured his heart out to Jastrow. The resort, he explained, was in horrible shape. Ownership hadn't spent much money on the golf course. There was no marketing to speak of. Meanwhile Pebble had been facing criticism for exploitative pricing of green fees, and the list went on.

"Tom said 'My business is way down. We have less than 50 percent occupancy and the perception and allure of Pebble Beach is completely gone,'" recalled Jastrow.

His request to Jastrow was simple: "When you telecast the Open can you manage to find a way to show The Lodge and talk about the experience here at Pebble more than just the 18 holes."

Jastrow obliged. If one goes back and revisits the opening shots of ABC's Open telecast, one will find unapologetic paeans to the comfort and luxury of life at The Lodge.

"I started with a tight shot of the front door of The Lodge," says Jastrow, "and pulled back to the first tee with the announcer saying 'Only 50 yards from the magnificent Lodge at Pebble Beach lies the first tee ... '" Oliver later told Jastrow that after the Saturday and Sunday telecasts, the phones lit up as never before. Pebble started filling rooms and was able to put some money back into the golf course.

"The Open made Pebble Beach, in terms of room rates and occupancy," said Frank Hannigan.

CHAPTER 6

In This Corner

AT 74 YEARS OLD, Watson is still prodigiously long. Unlike so many senior swings that have become shorter, stubbier, or quicker with age, Tom's move still has that precise seesaw timing that served him so well for so long. His short game, in particular his putting, has come and gone a handful of times, but his youthful competitiveness and his cherubic appearance are still redolent of his greatest years. Aside from the leathery neck, the hide-worn hands, and a few well-placed wrinkles, Watson still resembles the all-American boy from Kansas.

In the post-war 1940s, the Sunflower State was ground zero for American values. Watson was born in 1949 of a distinguished family. His father, Raymond, was in the insurance business, which would long loom as a career fallback for young Watson. A very skilled amateur player (he holds the amateur course record of 64 at Kansas City Country Club; son, Tom, holds the professional record of 60), Raymond was a huge U.S. Open fan and had an encyclopedic knowledge of the championship. He could name every U.S. Open champion by year going back to 1895 and provide details on the win. He was intensely competitive, a trait he studiously ingrained in Tom.

"Like so many other players, my dad taught me how to play the game," said Watson in an insightful 2023 podcast discussion with hosts Bruce Devlin and Mike Gonzalez. "He taught me how to grip the club and told me to finish with my belly button facing the hole. This was his first lesson to me."

Not long afterwards, Raymond had his six-year-old son working the ball. "He got a big kick out of teaching me how to hook it and slice it. Here I am, a six-year-old kid, when I learned how to curve the ball. That's how my dad taught me the game, he had a great passion for it."

As a child Tom would beat balls around the hilly fairways of the Kansas City Country Club, and chip and putt for hours on end. Golf professional Stan Thirsk first saw Watson's potential at a pitching, chipping, and putting contest in 1955 at the Mission Hills Country Club.

"He was six years old, a little freckle-faced kid that spit through the gap in his teeth like his father did," Thirsk told an interviewer in 1996, "but he had the most beautiful balance you ever saw for a kid."

Ray put his son in Thirsk's capable hands with one simple command: copy Sam Snead's swing. On Saturday afternoons Thirsk and Ray Watson would teach Tom how to compete. "The Watsons would challenge me to play against their best ball," said Thirsk in a wide-ranging 1983 article in *Stanford Magazine*. "Ray was a great negotiator and he would structure the bet so that if Tom played well he could just beat me."

By 12 the youngster started spending Mondays competing with and against local teaching pros. The outings were put together by Thirsk, who was not only a legendary teacher, but an excellent player who competed in more than a dozen major championships.

"Stan would call the house and say, 'Tommy, you wanna

come out and play with us pros this Monday?' "Young Watson who had been bred with an appetite for history, jumped at the chance, and throughout his early teens he eagerly joined these groups. The pros would gamble and drink, Watson soaking it all in. "That's how I grew up," said Watson, "inside the curtain."

Young Watson was a standout. Four times he won the Missouri State Amateur. Four-times he won the state high school championship. He was an all-around athlete, but Watson, much like the man he would battle down the stretch at Pebble Beach, was attracted less to a given sport than to the concept of competition. The quarterback of his high school football team, who also played varsity basketball and golf, Watson was a ferocious competitor. In fact, golf's gain was baseball's loss.

Watson had an abiding love for the national pastime. He was a huge fan of Mickey Mantle, Whitey Ford, Yogi Berra, Bob Feller, Sandy Koufax, and Don Drysdale. When Watson was 8 years old he played for a local youth team that was sponsored by The Hen House, a local grocery chain. "With a sheepish laugh Watson recalls, "We were called the Hen House Chicks." With a good arm and good speed, but a slow bat, Watson's baseball career waned, leaving summers open for...something else. "I basically concentrated on playing golf. I had another game to play and my dad belonged to a club that I could play and practice at."

He won the Kansas City match play championship as a 14-year-old.

Ray also arranged for his son to play with various professional golfers as they came through Kansas City and by the time young Watson had graduated from Pembroke Country Day School in 1969, he had already gone head-to-head in exhibition matches against both Arnold Palmer and Jack Nicklaus.

"That's something most people don't notice about Tom," said Thirsk, who died in 2015. "He has a disarming little smile that television announcers say makes him look like Huck Finn. But he fools people with it. Tom may have a grin on his face but inside he's saying to himself 'I'm going to drill this guy.'"

Despite young Watson's outsized athletic talent, he never envisioned a career as a professional athlete. Watson had long planned on a career in business or insurance with a sideline in amateur competition. In fact, as hard as it is to believe in this day and age of collegiate Tour-player factories, Watson entered Stanford University (where his father and two brothers studied) without a golf scholarship.

"I didn't go to Stanford to further my golf career," said Watson. There were a lot of other responsibilities and distractions for me. I had come from Kansas City, where discipline is ingrained, to Stanford, where an individual had total freedom. During college I was always searching to improve myself, but finding the right direction wasn't easy."

Watson's collegiate game was a study in strengths and weaknesses. He was a startlingly long but often wild driver of the ball (in 1969 he won the NCAA long-drive championship with a persimmon-fueled blast of 298 yards). His Stanford teammates recall him as a remarkable putter, a characteristic that helped him make a name on the PGA Tour (only to desert him in later years). But what stood out about Watson early on were two qualities that had nothing to do with his swing or his putting stroke. Watson was unmatched in his intensity and his resiliency.

"He was a perfectionist," said Gary Vanier, his roommate

in the Alpha Sigma Phi fraternity house and second man to Watson on the golf team. "He was always very mechanically minded and would make little changes in his swing trying to make it perfect. He would hit balls on the range for hours while the rest of us would be out on the course playing. Tom is extremely competitive. You can see it playing ping-pong or basketball or anything else with him. He always wants to beat you."

In order to win Watson had to learn to recover from monstrously errant tee balls, which came, like clockwork, one or two to a round.

"Tom would be playing along really well and then he'd just knock it off the earth," Vanier said. These misses invariably cost Watson several penalty shots. His response: Complete composure. Simply re-tee and move on. This coolness, combined with a killer instinct and a deep reservoir of athletic skill, led Stanford head golf coach Bud Finger to write this remarkably prescient comment about "Tommy Watson" in the 1970 Stanford Golf Team press guide: "Awesome distance off the tee but also is a sharp iron player, accurate with the wedge and is a deadly putter. He could rise out of the college ranks to become one of the world's great players, just like Arnold Palmer, Jack Nicklaus, etc."

As skilled and as focused as he was, Watson barely registered on the national collegiate scene. Back then the Texas twins, Ben Crenshaw and Tom Kite, were the dominant forces in collegiate golf. In fact, the man who would go on to win more professional majors than Vardon, Sarazen, Snead, Palmer, Trevino, Faldo, and Nelson, would only win two collegiate tournaments in his four years in Palo Alto. Aside from earning second-team all-America honors in 1969, '70 and '71, Watson was largely off the radar. Often alone and occa-

sionally with a group of teammates he would drive from Palo
Alto to Pebble Beach early in the morning. Teeing off around
7 a.m., he'd play a quick 36 holes; re-play holes 1 through 5,
and then cut across to the 14th and play in from there. While
playing those last few holes Watson would play-act the fan-
tasy of every youngster who picked up a club in the 1960s or
1970s: taking on the great Jack Nicklaus. Unlike most kids'
dreams, Watson's had a foundation in future reality.

"I'd say to myself, 'You've got to play these holes 1-un-
der to win the Open.' Of course, I'd always play them 2-over.
Then I'd think to myself, 'You've got a long way to go, kid.'"

Watson arrived in Palo Alto a liberal-leaning econom-
ics major. He actually voted for George McGovern in 1972
(When he told his conservative father about the ballot the
stone-faced reply came, "You are an idiot."). Collegiate golf,
even at venerated Stanford, was a far cry from the glam-fest it
is today. In a time when it's not at all unusual for NCAA pow-
erhouses such as Oklahoma State to travel to far-away tournaments in the comfort of a private jet, it's hard to believe
how decidedly unglamorous Pac-10 golf was in those days.
The Cardinal played in few tournaments, traveled very little
and in order to stay competitively sharp they even scheduled
matches against local high school teams.

Watson played in three NCAA Tournaments. His best
finish would come in 1970 when the championship was contested at the Ohio State University's famed Scarlet Course.
the University of Houston won the team title and their star,
John Mahaffey, took the individual title. Watson finished
fifth.

Watson would graduate with a degree in psychology, and
halfway through his senior year he made another change,
this time to his career plan. Rather than remain an amateur

and follow his father into the business world, Watson decided to pursue a career in professional golf. The decision was based on Watson's typically Midwestern pragmatism: "I was no great shakes as a student," he confessed. "My golf game was the only tangible talent I thought I had." And by 1971 he knew that the talent ran deep. Before going off to Q-school Watson would tell friends back in Kansas, "I want to be the best golfer in the world."

But as the 1970s wore on he would face a number of obstacles to that distinction, chief among them his own errant play (particularly in the U.S. Open) and a guy named Jack Nicklaus.

Whereas Nicklaus' rise to greatness had all the drama of a slow-moving steamroller, Watson's climb was a remarkable series of ups and downs, stunning wins and searing setbacks. But just like the youngster back in Stanford who would calmly re-tee and play on after bombing a ball "off the earth" and out of play, Watson would bounce back. For example, a month after his head-shaking collapse in the 1975 U.S. Open at Medinah, he traveled to windy, rainy Carnoustie and won the British Open in his first appearance in the fabled championship.

Despite his early successes, particularly in non-U.S. Open play, Watson the mechanic was constantly tweaking his swing. In the kind of perfectionist pursuit that eventually did in the careers of contemporaries Tom Weiskopf and Bert Yancey, and that would temper the great Nick Faldo in the 1990s, Watson baffled many by trifling with his classic and repeating swing. By the mid-1970s Watson had come to believe that the upright swing he had used since childhood was the cause of his wildness with the driver. In particular, Watson felt it was forcing his wayward shots to the right. In 1975 and '76 he began to flatten his swing with regrettable results. In 1976, for the first time since turning professional, Watson earned less money than he did the previous year. Frustration, even embarrassment, ensued. Watson actually failed to qualify for the final 18 holes of the 1976 British Open, the defense of his '75 crown. Worse, he would go winless that year for the first time in three seasons.

The 1977 campaign was a turning point for the still-young Watson. He would win early in the year at The Crosby at Pebble Beach and The Andy Williams in San Diego. But only a few weeks later he would blow big final-round leads at TPC and at Hilton Head. Watson was becoming known more for his failures than for his accomplishments. He was labeled a "choker." That year at The Masters, Watson was tied with Ben Crenshaw for the 54-hole lead. Seven players, including Nicklaus, were within four shots. Watson was asked which player he was most worried about. His answer, conditioned by his spate of recent collapses was honest, if uninspiring. "The person I fear most on the last two rounds is myself," said Watson. Remarkably, he would go on to a two-stroke win in a famed seesaw battle with Nicklaus. It was a rebirth for Watson and the birth of a rivalry that would dazzle and delight the game's fans for the next five years.

The second installment of Watson-Nicklaus would unfold at Turnberry that July. After 54 holes Watson and Nicklaus were tied for the lead. Both shot identical rounds of 68-70-65 to share a three-shot lead going into the final round. On Sunday, Nicklaus made four birdies in the first 12 holes for a two-shot lead with six holes to play. Watson then went on a memorable tear of his own, birdieing three of the next five and taking a one-shot lead into the 18th. On the par-four home hole Watson hit a 1-iron off the tee, then a 7-iron to two feet of the hole. Nicklaus who drove the ball in gorse on the right, miraculously chopped it out to 35 feet and in his Nicklausian way, managed to intimidate his birdie putt into the hole. The two at least briefly were tied, but when the 28-year-old Watson coolly holed his two-footer he had again disposed of the 37-year-old Golden Bear.

The argument has been made that one of the reasons Tiger Woods so dominated the global golf scene from 1997 through 2009 was a dearth of legitimate opposition. There are undoubtedly more great players today than at any time in the game's long history. But among the contenders at the very pinnacle of the game during Tiger's reign—the elite players such as Phil Mickelson, Sergio Garcia, Padraig Harrington, Ernie Els, Vijay Singh, Adam Scott, Geoff Ogilvy, Jose Maria Olazabal, Greg Norman, and David Duval going back to the late 1990s—none managed to either psychologically or competitively get in Woods' kitchen. In fact, the reverse is true. Most observers concede that Woods attained psychological as well physical mastery over his opponents. Between 1997, his first full year on tour, and the 2008 U.S. Open at Torrey Pines, Woods won 14 major championships. His closest peers over that period won a combined total of 12.

Contrast that with the opposition Nicklaus faced in the 1960s from Arnold Palmer, Billy Casper, and Gary Player; in the '70s from Player, Tom Weiskopf, Lee Trevino, Raymond Floyd, Watson, and even into the early 1980s from Watson, Tom Kite, Hale Irwin, and Greg Norman. Between 1962 and 1986 Jack Nicklaus won 18 professional majors. His most prominent rivals won a combined total of 31.

In his early years, few players rattled Nicklaus more palpably than Palmer. The Golden Bear has admitted Palmer's very presence in a field often cost Nicklaus valuable strokes.

When Palmer was around, Nicklaus, who became famous for his impenetrable concentration, spent valuable energy trying to keep up with his rival instead of tending to his own game. In later years, particularly the late 1960s and early 1970s, Trevino inherited the mantle of head Bear-baiter. The Merry Mex's incessant on-course banter, his less-than-classic swing and, most of all, his genius for the mind-game, were the undoing of Nicklaus in majors such as the 1968 U.S. Open at Oak Hill, the 1971 edition at Merion (where on the first tee prior to their Monday playoff Trevino playfully pulled a toy rubber snake from his bag and tossed it at Nicklaus), and the 1972 British Open at Muirfield.

As the 1970s wore on Watson became the new Lee Trevino. He possessed that rare touch of Kryptonite that could undo the great Nicklaus. In fact, after losing the British Open at Turnberry, Nicklaus seemed to have discovered first-hand what Watson's teammates at Stanford had known for a decade: Watson was both a physical and mental force. "His mental edge may set Tom apart from everyone else," said Nicklaus afterwards. He added, in terms that could have described himself in his prime, "He's the strongest thinker of the lot. He's got a positive manner. He knows where he's going—as if he had blinders on."

Those precise traits, along with obscene amounts of power, are what brought Nicklaus to god-like stature in the late 1970s. Like a feudal lord, he commanded the golf landscape for as far as the eye could see. There were occasional uprisings. Trevino, Weiskopf, Miller, Bruce Crampton, and Hubert Green would win the occasional battle, but Nicklaus was dominating the war. In the two decades spanning from 1962 (when he turned professional) to 1982 (when he would battle Watson at Pebble Beach) 80 major championships were contested. Nicklaus won 15 of them and finished in the top 5 a total of 49 times.

His specialty was the U.S. Open. Yes, Nicklaus cornered the market on Kelly-green fabric as the only six-time winner of the Masters, but all along he knew that the toughest championship to win was the U.S. Open, and by 1980 he had joined the small group of men who had won four of them. Nicklaus' reverence for the U.S. Open and his success in the championship is not surprising given that the Open, specifically the 1926 edition, served as a backdrop for his very entry into the sport.

Fourteen years before Nicklaus was born Bobby Jones won the U.S. Open at Scioto Country Club in Columbus, Ohio. Jones' win had a lasting impact on locals and members who for decades afterwards, would point out to one another and guests the spots from which Jones had played each of his 293 shots. Among the eyewitnesses to Jones' victory was Nicklaus' father, 13-year-old Charlie Nicklaus, who watched every shot Jones played that week. His affection for Jones and the romance of the U.S. Open were passed on to Charlie's only son, Jack William Nicklaus, at a very early age. The inheritance affected young Nicklaus' entire outlook on the game, particularly his unmitigated regard for the national championship. Nicklaus has always rated the majors in this order of importance: U.S. Open, British Open, PGA Championship, and The Masters. Driving his regard for the American Open are the quality of U.S. Open courses, their set-up and conditioning, the quality of the field, and "the fact that, as an American, it is the championship of my country. I also believe it is the toughest of the four to win."

By 1982, Jack Nicklaus had easily emerged as the most dominant force in modern Open history with four U.S.

Opens (one at Pebble Beach in 1972). He had lost the U.S. Open the previous year to Lee Trevino in the snake-aided playoff at Merion. The Open was pure golf, pure difficulty, pure Nicklaus. Many times Nicklaus has remarked on how he prefers tougher set-ups as they thinned the field for him. The Masters may have been his personal playground, but the U.S. Open was Nicklaus' crucible, the vessel in which his talent was vulcanized. He came to the California coast in search of an unprecedented fifth U.S. Open title, an accomplishment that would have edged him beyond the elite company of Jones, Ben Hogan, and Willie Anderson. Oddly, just as Watson needed an Open for validation, Nicklaus needed one for posterity.

Watson was as devoted an Open suitor as Nicklaus, but had nothing to show for it. Surely, he could beat Nicklaus in a major championship, but in a U.S. Open? At Pebble Beach? They had competed often on nameless faceless Tour venues, and even stately major championships, but now they were essentially fighting for the same girl—the national championship they both prized on the course they both loved.

CHAPTER 7

"It's Only Cable"

GOLF AND TELEVISION are a perfect match. Because the pace of tournament action is unfettered by a clock, the viewing is leisurely and the insertion of advertising can be done with some flexibility. Combine mellow announcers with pastoral settings and you can understand how Barcalounger stays in business.

Even though golf, television, and the easy chair share a deep history, it wasn't always as easy as it looks. Even with the most advanced equipment, most television producers agree that live golf is the most difficult sport to televise. Where the activity in a football, basketball, baseball, hockey, or tennis competition takes place between the predictable confines of a court or a field and features anywhere from two to 22 players, the canvas of action for a golf tournament can comprise hundreds of acres and feature dozens of players. Unlike the time limits in clock-based sports such as hockey and basketball, a round of championship golf begins at dawn and ends (or at least stops) at dusk. Add leaders and contenders who may be several holes (even miles) apart and the difficulty of tracking a ball that is 1.68 inches in diameter and moving at a hundred-plus miles an hour over hundreds of acres of grass and foliage, and you get the idea.

During a distinguished career at KSD-TV in St. Louis, Keith Gunther produced all kinds of programs from symphonies to wrestling to golf. "Golf," he said in an interview for this book, "is probably the most difficult of all sports to direct." He should know. Gunther produced the game's first telecast. Fittingly, given how the Open would push the envelope of televised golf in years to come, the first golf tournament ever televised was a U.S. Open, the 1947 edition at St. Louis County Club. Compared to the digital ease of today's productions, the '47 Open was a man-sized struggle.

The plan called for 12 men and two stationary Image-Orthicon cameras (one with a 15-inch lens, the other with a 24-inch lens) mounted atop a specially designed RCA mobile unit truck, which was parked behind the 18th green. Pile on extreme heat, and it was real work.

"Well, you had to string the coaxial cable all over the place, setting up the power source and all that. It was a very big undertaking for the engineering department to put all this together, both the video and the audio," said Gunther, who passed away in 2015. "The biggest problem was stringing the cable and having enough power and efficient power for all of it."

It sounds almost prehistoric now, but the black and white images were relayed by coaxial cable from the mobile unit to a relay transmitter on the roof of the clubhouse several hundred feet away. From there shots of legends such as Ben Hogan, Byron Nelson, and Sam Snead (who would lose by 2 in a playoff to Lew Worsham) were beamed to the KSD transmitter atop the downtown headquarters of the *St. Louis Post-Dispatch*. From there the broadcast was disseminated locally as well as to NBC Television Network headquarters in New York. Audio commentary, the first ever for televised championship golf, was provided by Grams and the KSD sports director, Bob Ingham. During periods of inaction—and with only the 18th hole to show, there were plenty of them—KSD's director of special news events, Frank Eschen, set up shop outside the scorer's tent and did a turn as gadfly interviewer, collaring notables such as Francis Ouimet and USGA president Charles Littlefield. Several players actually made the trip to KSD's downtown studio for extended post-round chatter and golf tips.

"You had action taking place all over, and our communications were rather rudimentary as far as keeping the production team and the viewers up to date on who was in the lead, who wasn't, who was on the green, etc.," said Gunther. "With limited facilities it was very difficult to present a cohesive program."

Gunther says that while glitches were routine the players were largely oblivious to the electronics experiment unfolding around them, at least during play.

"No, they didn't give a damn about it," he said. "Television was just not that important an element in the game. It was immaterial to them."

Unless, of course, there was a buck to be made.

"I asked the little fella, Ben Hogan. I asked him to do an interview," said Gunther, "and he was a little bit testy and he said, 'Well, if you pay me x-number of dollars I'll do it.' I said, 'No, no we don't pay for that kind of thing.'"

The audience response, to the extent that a response could be elicited from a city that had about 300 televisions, was positive, says Gunther, who confessed to a rather low bar. "There was always a rather good response to anything we did because television was such a unique attraction. We could have put a refrigerator on air and opened and closed the door and we would have drawn a crowd."

Today's golf telecasts, no matter how technically advanced, are all built on the KSD model. Over time technology has made it possible to cover more ground, but even as late as the mid-1960s only a sliver of the potential action was covered. For instance, when ABC Sports aired its first U.S. Open in 1966—a championship infamous for Arnold Palmer's Olympic-sized collapse—their coverage began at the 15th hole.

According to Terry Jastrow, long-time director of golf telecasts for ABC Sports, fans of golf, in particular fans of the U.S. Open, who have grown accustomed to enjoying expanded coverage actually, have the U.S. Open and Pebble Beach to thank.

It was early 1972 when Jastrow and the ABC staff and engineers headed out to Pebble Beach to scout the course and determine camera locations for ABC's broadcast of that June's U.S. Open, the first to be played at Pebble. Jastrow, his executive producer Chuck Howard, and their boss Roone Arledge were intimately familiar with the course from their many broadcasts of the old Crosby Clambake. Even those telecasts began late in the back nine, but in 1972, "because it was the Open and because it was Pebble" Jastrow said the network began to view the layout with fresh eyes.

"We always felt evolution in sports television and especially golf television would come by pushing the envelope for the national championship of American golf," said Jastrow. "We absolutely pushed every envelope we could find to make coverage of the U.S. Open bigger, better, more spectacular, and more comprehensive."

While patrolling the course to decide on camera locations, etc., Jastrow and Howard fell in love with the series of early holes that (aside from the 5th hole which had to maneuver inland around the infamous Beatty property) head to the sea. "Pebble breaks out on to the ocean at Hole 4 and then you see 6, 7, 8, 9, and 10," says Jastrow. "During The Crosby we didn't come on the air until the 14th hole, but this was the Open, and we couldn't stand to not show those holes. We were so hungry to get that on the air."

Howard and Jastrow called Arledge from Pebble Beach with a big idea: expand coverage of the U.S. Open from the last five holes to the last 14 or 15 holes. "We said 'Roone, we know it pushes our coverage back, but we've gotta figure out a way," recalled Jastrow.

Arledge knew all about Pebble. He was not only an avowed golf nut with a considerable expense account, but he had played in several Crosbys as the partner of none other than Tom Weiskopf. "He knew exactly what we were talking about," said Jastrow.

Asking Arledge if he wants more Pebble Beach is like asking Christopher Walken if he wants more cowbell. The only problem was that in order to air the expanded coverage, ABC would need to snatch two hours from contiguous programming. The answer was quickly obvious: Arledge's brainchild, Wide World of Sports was slated to precede ABC's Saturday U.S. Open telecast. Arledge decided to present the early-hole coverage as part of Wide World. "We got the hours off Wide World of Sports," said Jastrow. "And that's how we came on the air to show those great early holes at Pebble."

The lessons of their experiment taught the producers and engineers (and likely the ad sales staff) that "we could come in much earlier on a golf course, start much earlier, and get in more holes," said Jastrow. Eventually, five years later at the 1977 Open at Southern Hills, ABC did what was once unthinkable: Air all 18 holes both days of a major championship weekend. Now 18-hole coverage of major championships is becoming routine. "What led to it all," said Jastrow, "are those magnificent holes at Pebble."

Unless you were alive and a sports fan in the 1960s and 1970s it's difficult to describe how influential ABC Sports was. Ask any male over the age of 40 (one who knows the difference between a ball and a strike) to hum the fanfare-laden theme song from Wide World of Sports. Then ask him to sing a song from his wedding. That was the power of ABC Sports. Far too big to be called a cult, the ABC Sports of the '60s and '70s and even into the 1980s would best be described as a religion. On weekend afternoons Wide World was where buddies and fathers and sons and uncles (and even a smattering of moms and sisters) gathered to see *The Encyclopedia of Sports* merge with the Michelin travel guide. Not a single American woke up on a Saturday in the 1970s wondering about Scandinavian barrel-jumpers or Mexican cliff divers, but Arledge's Wide World transported viewers' imaginations and broadened their view. One glimpse of those garish yellow announcers' blazers and ice bike polo was suddenly as real and as compelling as the World Series.

Much of the show's (and the network's) success can be attributed to Arledge's vision—his belief—that, with the right mix of personal insight and close-up camera shots, the participants would become as important, or maybe even more important than the sport. In Arledge's view, one that would come to its fullest evolution in his famed "Up Close and Personal" treatment of the Olympic Games, once the audience had formed a bond with the athlete, the activity was almost irrelevant.

The conduit between those of us laying on orange shag rugs at home and those crazy cliff-divers in Acapulco was the likable, reliable, ever-present everyman anchorman, Jim McKay. In a documentary tribute to McKay, who died in 2008 at the age of 86, NBC Sports Chairman Dick Ebersol, who worked for Arledge in the late 1960s and early 1970s, said that Wide World and McKay could work their magic on anyone. "In demolition derby," Ebersol once said, "Jim actually made you feel for the guy who was about to barrel ass-backwards into the other guy."

Wide World became the face of the country's predominant authority on televised sports. The acclaim and profitability of ABC's sports division would put the young network on the map. And in a case of backwards maturation, ABC's sports department provided the network's news and entertainment divisions solid lead-ins and ratings credibility. By the late 1960s, the ABC television network—the youngest of the Big Three and the one that had strained longest for credibility—was without peer. CBS may have had football and the Masters, and NBC had baseball and some pigskin, but ABC had Roone Arledge. It was essentially the Arledge Broadcasting Company.

In a 1968 profile of Arledge for the *New York Times*, the paper's TV critic wrote that "in eight years at ABC, during which he went from producer, a rank somewhat above office boy, to president in charge of a $65 million a-year budget, he brought the network from the cellar to the dome of the television sports business, turning a competitive pussycat into the kind of beast that the other denizens of the network jungle … treat with wary respect."

Terry Jastrow first began working for ABC in 1968 while still a student at the University of Houston. Working for

Chris Millard

Arledge in golf at ABC Sports was like working for Willy Wonka at the chocolate factory.

"Roone did a lot to bring the sports division of ABC and the network into parity with the other networks. So no one really screwed around with us too much," said Jastrow. We were making a lot of money. We were pioneering in lots of different ways. And Roone always loved golf."

Even with the decision by ABC to expand coverage, the 1972 Open at Pebble was a surprisingly dicey proposition. There was the previously discussed distance from a major metro populace. Secondly, because of its heavy play the "public" course was saddled with conditioning problems; and, finally, prior to 1972 no U.S. Open had ever been staged on a public golf course.

Of course, the USGA needn't have worried. Jack Nicklaus, who had won the U.S. Amateur at Pebble in 1961, dropped the hammer on Bruce Crampton in 1972. Nicklaus not only won his third Open title, but also launched Pebble Beach into irreversible acclaim.

If the 1972 Open was decisive in terms of its influence on Pebble Beach and televised golf, the 1982 Open was a landmark in the history of sports television period. It marked not only the beginning of extended live golf coverage, but it was the first time that golf was broadcast in the United States on a weekday. Most significantly, the '82 Open marked the first golf tournament ever produced by ABC Sports' for what was then derogatorily referred to as "cable," specifically, a lowly and financially unstable Rube-Goldbergian all-sports wannabe. It was rather blandly dubbed the Entertainment Sports Programming Network and located in media hotbed Bristol, Connecticut.

71

While it may have looked simple enough at the time—broadcast old-boy throwing an upstart cable network a bone—the shift of early-round U.S. Open coverage to what would become ESPN represented the advent of a tectonic movement in mass media. If one wanted to pinpoint the precise moment that the old tri-network model of broadcast sports television began to cede to the new hyper-narrow model of cable sports television—in particular the oxygen-stealing rise of ESPN—this was it. The decision by ABC brass to have ABC Sports staff produce the first two rounds of the 1982 Open for ESPN to air did three things: It foreshadowed the decline of heralded ABC Sports; it christened the future of cable sports "narrow-casting"; and it provided an object lesson in the financial clout afforded cable's dual revenue streams (subscriber fees plus advertising for cable networks vs. only advertising for broadcast networks).

In 1982 cable television was still a relatively new concept, but it was growing. In 1978, only 17 percent of American households had cable. By 1989, cable penetration had reached 57 percent. Still, from virtually any standpoint—artistic, aesthetic, creative, programming, rights packages—cable networks were the redheaded stepchildren of broadcast TV. Only a few years prior to 1982, ESPN's founder, Bill Rasmussen, was traversing the country in a van pushing the concept on reluctant advertisers. In 1978 Rasmussen, a former radio sports reporter and avowed sports nut, lost his job as director of communications for the old World Hockey Association's Hartford Whalers. He began looking into creating a cable net focused on sports in Connecticut. His original idea was to buy blocks of time, late-night or early-morning, on an existing cable net, but in a quirk that opened the door to the most successful network launch in history, he found it would be cheaper for the cash-starved start-up to buy 24/7 satellite access than it would be to buy chunks of time on existing networks. But at 24 hours-a-day (back then even the big three networks didn't air round the clock, and CNN didn't even exist), this thing wouldn't be cheap. Rasmussen needed investors. In late 1978 Rasmussen, whose passion for sports had spurred the idea, was about to bail. It was then that Getty Oil stepped up and invested $20.6 million in the concept (other investors, including Anheuser-Busch would soon follow suit).

But what to put on the air? The major professional sports leagues had long ago sold their rights to the big three broadcast networks, CBS, NBC, and ABC. All that remained for ESPN was the leftovers, overlooked morsels of undercooked "sports" such as Australian Rules Football and professional wrestling. Not exactly the NFL. In fact, when ESPN debuted at 7 p.m. on September 7, 1979 from a mobile unit in a muddy lot, the first programming to appear on the network, SportsCenter, was followed by a professional slow-pitch softball game between the Kentucky Bourbons and the Milwaukee Schlitz.

Still, few outside of Bristol or St. Louis or Getty Oil took ESPN seriously. Steve Anderson, who would become an executive vice president of ESPN, was hired by the network in 1980, only months after the net's inauspicious debut. At the time, even he saw the gangly start-up as nothing more than a place to get some experience before moving on to the real thing. "I came to ESPN in April of 1980 as an SA (sports associate), even lower than a PA (production associate), to get experience so that I could get a job in NYC with one of the three networks ... There are people who will tell you now that they knew ESPN was going to become a player, but that it would become what it's become? That things would unfold like this? I wasn't even sure we were gonna make it."

The fledgling network made its first foray into big-time sports when, in March of 1980, it aired early-rounds of the NCAA basketball tournament. As hard as it is to believe today—an era when March Madness lasts most of a month and can better be described as March Adness—in the early 1980s the early round NCAA games were considered tripe, table scraps.

"When we first started televising the first two rounds of the NCAA, nobody had thought about putting all of those games on," said Anderson, who played basketball at Holy Cross and ended up working on the NCAA hoop package, "and to hear how excited fans were that these games were now available was like, hmm, maybe we're on to something."

The network's college pact was followed by a two-year deal (1982-84) with the NBA. The cable net had stabilized and caught the attention of ABC, which acquired a majority stake in ESPN in 1984.

It's hard to describe the cultural schism that existed between broadcast and cable at the time. Frank Hannigan, the long-time USGA man had, among his responsibilities, managing the Association's relationships and contracts with broadcasters. In fact, in 1977, Hannigan raised a few eyebrows when as the USGA's nebulously-titled director of special projects, he joined the on-air staff of ABC Sports which had rights to the USGA's championships. There was an obvious conflict of interest there, one to which Hannigan readily admitted, but the dual perch did give him a front-row seat to the class warfare between the broadcast haves and the cable have-nots.

"People at ABC had a very low regard for ESPN's production abilities," said Hannigan in a 2004 interview. "This is before ESPN had all the money."

Chuck Howard was an executive producer at ABC. If Arledge was God, Howard was Peter. Like most ABC staffers of the time, Howard looked down his nose not simply at ESPN, but at all of cable. In fact, says longtime ABC Sports golf statistician Sal Johnson, who worked for Howard at the time, "He thought cable was a fad." Johnson adds that Thursday morning of the 1982 Open, hours before his work would be diverted through cables rather than airwaves, Howard sardonically said to his staff, "Hey, check to see if ESPN is still in business, maybe we won't have to do the show."

Jastrow who worked more closely with Howard than anyone at ABC, admits to a certain anti-cable bias. "We were aware of ESPN in sports television," he says, "but it was considered worse than local television, like the local affiliate in Des Moines."

Jastrow and Howard sat in meetings with the cable cowboys and wondered a la Butch and Sundance: Who are these guys? "Entertainment and Sports? ESPN? It stands for what? None of us could figure it out."

In the early 1980s, years before ABC would acquire ESPN, the cable net began to get interested in golf, and according to Jastrow, Roone Arledge got interested in ESPN "because he was always a step ahead of all of us. And when they came to talk to Roone and Chuck Howard about doing Thursday/ Friday coverage of the '82 Open, I remember Chuck came to me and it was like, Whoa."

Jastrow recalls a subsequent meeting "with these guys in our mobile unit, and I remember there was a bunch of guys from Getty, and I was trying to figure it all out: Getty Oil and

Getty owns ESPN? And I was really thinking these guys are just here for the hospitality room and the food. Then they said, 'We just want to put your rehearsal on the air.'"

Such a deal would mean that instead of working under live broadcast pressure for only Saturday and Sunday, the ABC Sports staff would be producing Thursday and Friday rounds for air with no additional pay. This was important not only from a morale standpoint, but from a quality control point of view. Thursday and Friday rounds used to be rehearsal days during which ABC staff could test camera angles and all other aspects under semi-live conditions. If the ESPN deal came about, Jastrow and Howard would forfeit two days of rehearsal.

Ben Harvey, who was an associate producer for ABC during the '82 Open, said, "We lost two days of off-air practice. We typically would have spent Thursday and Friday getting ready for Sunday. Now our rehearsals were on air and we couldn't be as good as we wanted to be right out of the gate."

Jastrow and Howard weighed the pros and cons as well as the fact that in the end Arledge was going to have his way. "Do we really want to start out there two days earlier and do all these hours for these guys for no money?" Then again, he added, "You wouldn't do the World Series and pick up at Game 3, you'd start at the beginning which (in the U.S. Open) was Thursday."

There was talk about bringing in other cameramen and other directors, but by then Jastrow and Howard had bought in. "We said nope, we'll do it. We'll do it happily."

Jimmy Roberts is now an Emmy Award-winning member of NBC Sports' on-air team, but in 1982 he was a puka-shell wearing production assistant for ABC Sports. He recalled that the news of ABC's deal with ESPN was not embraced by his colleagues. "It was going to be an enormous amount of work for us," said Roberts. "Basically our workload had been doubled. The directors and producers didn't take it well. They weren't going to do it. There was even talk of a strike."

Chuck Howard, who died in 1996, is one of the legends of sports television production. The mention of his name still stirs both fear and affection in the hearts of former ABC staffers, many of whom have gone on to highly successful careers. Howard was a complete perfectionist and a hard driver; some might even say he was downright mean.

There were several camps at ABC Sports, each one coming under the supervision of the network's three executive producers, Dennis Lewin, Chuck Howard, and Chet Forte. Each staffer fell into one of the camps. Roberts, a recent university of Maryland grad, became "a Chuck person because I had been hired by a Chuck person. And he took an interest in me, but that wasn't always a good thing," said Roberts. "He expected perfection and even though I got yelled at a lot, he taught me a lot. He taught me to at least strive for perfection. He would say, 'Why would you aim for anything less. Why would you try to be anything less than your best? At least try. If you don't attain it, don't beat yourself up"—Chuck would take care of that part.

"I was scared of him," said Roberts. "He screamed. He yelled. He struck fear into all of our souls. He was irrational a lot of times. He was incredibly opinionated."

Howard's trademark rant—"You don't have a clue!"—was spoken with such force that the words seemed to stick on recipients' skin. In fact, the young ABC staffers of the 1980s referred to getting yelled at by Howard as "getting tattooed." At the very least Howard was an anachronism, a guy with working-man sensibilities caught in what was evolving into show-biz.

"He could be irascible for sure," said Jastrow. "He had a trigger-quick temper and he could rip into people in ways you would be shocked to hear."

There are few people who worked as many hours and produced as many telecasts with Howard as Jastrow, who admits that for all Howard's bombast, "I loved him, I hold him with the fondest memories. I got a couple layers of skin off my back because of him, but you know that what he had first and foremost in mind is the excellence of the telecast, and a high regard for the sport."

What was remarkable about Howard's success in golf television production was that A) he was never a golfer himself and B) the consensus of those who worked most closely with him was that he wasn't particularly creative. As Jastrow explains, "He was just smart and kind of had a machine-gun smart analytical mind."

Ben Harvey saw the same thing. "Chuck Howard had a remarkable feel for golf for a guy who never played golf. He understood the emotions of the game and the flow of the game without ever being a player himself. He had incredible instincts about what was going to happen and about what was important. He had remarkable ability with timing whether he was producing golf or badminton. He knew sports so well."

But Howard was brutal on his staff. He and his fellow production legend Chet Forte routinely shredded staffers for the smallest of errors. The nastiness was contagious, but, says Jastrow, Arledge turned a blind eye.

"I always sort of blamed Roone," said Jastrow. "He didn't stop it and he could have. When he didn't, in a de facto way, he approved it. A bunch of us young guys coming up as directors and producers drew the conclusion that this is how big-time directors and producers are supposed to be, I guess.

And that was the wrong signal, and there was a generation, and I am embarrassed to say I was one of them, who were much too aggressive, arrogant, difficult, all of that, and it took a few of us to decide that this is not the way to do it and cycle out if it."

But Howard's irascibility inspired nearly as much loyalty as fear. Said one ABC Sports staffer of the era, "Chuck was a raging maniac and a fool, but he was OUR raging maniac and fool."

Harvey says he wouldn't go so far as to call him a maniac, but explains that Howard "was very forceful. Very straight-forward. In today's era of political correctness, his M.O. wouldn't fly. But back then the old drill instructor approach was clearly in place."

Steve Anderson, who worked the 1982 Open telecast, said that Howard once "yelled at us because we were two minutes early for a meeting." All a young employee needed was to show up late for a meeting to get an earful, so said Anderson, "we got to this meeting about two minutes early. He was standing outside the truck having a conversation with somebody and we didn't even interrupt, we just stood within sight so he would know we were there on time. He yelled over at us, "The meeting starts at 2:00!"

If Howard was the non-golfing brutish bad cop, Jastrow was more the smooth talking, sweet-swinging good cop. Jastrow was raised in golf. He grew up with Tom Kite and "used to go down to Austin and study with Harvey Penick." In their high school years Jastrow and Kite played golf together all summer long, avoiding fellow local Ben Crenshaw because "first of all he was two or three years younger than us and because he could beat the shit out of us."

Jastrow worked as a runner for ABC Sports in the late 1960s while still in college at the University of Houston on a golf scholarship (his suite-mate at U of H was 1975 U.S. Open runner-up John Mahaffey). He would work events in Texas, such as the Colonial, and would occasionally travel out to Pebble Beach on student half-fare. There he would work the Crosby events and get a sip of the golf/TV sponsorship cocktail. "I used to hold the cue cards for Bing," said Jastrow. "3M, they were the sponsors and Bing had to do this welcome to the tournament and I would hold his cue cards."

After graduation Jastrow was hired by ABC Sports as a production assistant and quickly identified as "the Roone Arledge of his generation." In the mid-1970s, the dashing Jastrow quietly enrolled in an acting class. The cover story was that the class might hone his television direction, but Jastrow fell for the greasepaint. His secretary at ABC made excuses for her boss who was sneaking out to study with the legendary Lee Strasberg. He took some bit parts in off-Broadway shows and then in 1977 made an arrangement with ABC that allowed him to work as a freelance director of the network's sports telecasts while pursuing an acting career in Hollywood. There were guest shots on TV series such as Police Story, but the most lasting thing to come out of his flirtation with Hollywood was his wife.

It was here that he met the up-and-coming actress, Anne Archer. At the time, the stunning Archer was best known as the daughter of Marjorie Lord, who played Danny Thomas' wife on the popular 1960s sitcom *Make Room For Daddy*. Of course, Archer would ultimately become famous for her own role as the poutingly seductive and loyal spouse, Beth Gallagher, in *Fatal Attraction*.

They became if not Hollywood royalty at least West Coast nobility, a deliciously handsome mix of sports and stardom. *People Magazine* covered their wedding, writing that it "could not have had a more decorous setting: the Bel Air living room of the bride's mother, TV actress Marjorie (Make Room for Daddy) Lord. But when the minister intoned, 'Now kiss the bride,' a familiar voice from among the attendants snarled: "Lay one hand on that lady and I'll break your arm." The voice, as every startled celebrant knew, was that of ABC sportscaster Howard Cosell."

For Jastrow and Chuck Howard there was certainly some unease as the split distribution of the 1982 Open approached, but there was one soothing factor. The lead announcer working ESPN's coverage was Jim Simpson (Dr. Cary Middlecoff was the color analyst, other commentators included Skeeter Heath, Jim Thacker, Lou Palmer, and long-time *Golf Digest* editor, Nick Seitz). Howard and Simpson knew and liked one another. They had both worked for ABC in the early days of the maverick American Football League.

While the casting of Simpson was a plus for Howard, it became an issue for the USGA, who felt their brand would be ill-served by second-team on-air talent. In fact, according to Hannigan, when the USGA later renewed its contract with ABC the Association stipulated that there be no more B-list on-air talent, that announcers for USGA championships, even for rounds shown on ESPN, had to be the ABC network regulars.

The revolution began seconds before 4:00 Eastern Time on June 17, 1982. ABC engineers tied into the lines and satellites that fed to Bristol, Connecticut. Jastrow, ensconced in his swivel chair in the darkened ABC Sports mobile unit in Pebble Beach, intoned, "Get Bristol ready. 10 seconds to

Bristol." And 10 seconds later, with the words, "Bristol, ready, take it," a new era was launched. Jim Simpson's familiar tones offered viewers a hearty "Hello from Pebble Beach, California," and, with that, ESPN was in the business of broadcasting major championship golf.

No one in Bristol, New York City, or Pebble Beach could have known the import of the moment, but the switch had been turned on a new media model. As Jastrow explains, "it didn't take long to figure out that, wait a second, these guys (ESPN) are getting subscriber fees from cable systems, and they're charging for commercials, they're taking bites out of both these apples. You could figure that out, and a lot of smart people who paid attention to those things jumped on the bandwagon early. But frankly, in those days we regarded cable as a nuisance except when it came to them knocking on our door and saying, "hey how'd you like to get the early rounds of the U.S. Open?"

The flick of Howard's switch foreshadowed the beginning of the end for ABC's dominance in sports television. Like a battle-weary ship coming to port for decommission, Arledge's aircraft carrier would continue under its own momentum for another 20 years, but, in time, dual revenues, younger audiences and niche programming would undermine the staid broadcaster. There is no longer an ABC Sports. All the production and operations for sports programming airing on ABC are actually performed by ESPN. which has come a long way from the back of Bill Rasmussen's van. Now owned by Disney, the network counts 100 million subscribers and enjoys revenues of about $3 billion a year, more than the entire networks of ABC, NBC, and CBS combined.

Steve Anderson, who retired from ESPN in 2015, was asked if anyone at ESPN or ABC in 1982 could have predicted the rise of ESPN and the consequent evaporation of ABC Sports. "No way," he said. "Anybody who says they did is crazy."

The USGA's Hannigan concurred. "Trust me, nobody understood that ESPN would become this behemoth. I would say that only by the mid '90s it became apparent that ABC Sports would not exist for much more."

The late Frank Hannigan shared one lasting and rather telling recollection of those early cable/broadcast tension fests. He distinctly recalled the famed ABC broadcaster Jim McKay reminding the staff not to waste their good stuff on those Thursday/Friday ESPN telecasts, telling the troops, "Remember, it's only cable."

CHAPTER 8

Life and Death at the U.S. Open

IN JUNE OF 1982, Raymond Floyd was not the best golfer in the world, but he may have been the hottest. Coming into the U.S. Open at Pebble Beach, Raymund had won two of the previous three tournaments, the Memorial and the Danny Thomas Memphis Classic. His only rival in terms of raw heat was Craig Stadler, who had not only won the Masters in April, but the Kemper Open at the testing Congressional Country Club, a place where he and his fade always seemed to fare well.

Meanwhile, as Watson headed west to Pebble, he was at a crossroads. He was statistically the top player in the world, but he lacked a U.S. Open title. The U.S. Open meant something to Tom Watson. It meant plenty to millions of players, fans, broadcasters, writers, and caddies, too, but one can argue it meant more to Tom Watson than any of them. It had to do not only with the championship's place in golf history, but with the place of golf history in the Watson family. This was personal. Watson's father, Raymond, a conservative insurance executive in Kansas City and himself a very skilled amateur player, was a huge U.S. Open fan. He would name every U.S. Open champion going back to 1895, often at the dinner table, feeding bits of golf history to his sons like feeding chicks in a nest. Raymond's obsession with the Open rubbed off on his young son, as did the undercurrent of patriotism that inspired it.

By the time Watson arrived at Pebble he had already bagged five major championships (three British Opens and two Masters). He had already nudged aside the game's greatest players at several of the game's most challenging venues, but even monumental accomplishments like knocking off Nicklaus at both Augusta and Turnberry in 1977 had not earned Watson unanimous regard as the game's dominant player. He needed a U.S. Open championship not simply to round out a resume or convince doubters of his mastery; he needed a U.S. Open title for self-validation. Watson, who became aware of the U.S. Open as a toddler and had dreamed of winning the championship since he was 10 years old, said, "The Open is more important than any other tournament. To be a complete golfer you have to win the Open. You just have to."

He spoke placidly enough of his pursuit a few minutes before teeing off in the final that Sunday in 1982 at Pebble. "It's our national championship," he said. "It's one of our majors. I haven't won and it's a tournament I want to win very much." The words came out calmly enough, but Mel Brooks' film version would have had Watson twitching with each syllable.

Despite Watson's lifelong jones for the Open, the affection had not been returned. Pick the image—Sisyphus pushing the rock up the hill, Icarus flying too close to the sun, or Petrarch drowning in a pool of unrequited ardor—Watson seemed bedeviled, fated to fail in the event he cherished most. His Open bio read like a troubling EKG.

The first time Watson ever qualified for the U.S. Open was in 1972, when the competition was staged, ironically, at Pebble Beach. Watson, then 22 years old, would finish tied for 29th. For any other young Kansan playing in his first U.S. Open, this could be considered a solid debut. But Watson knew the golf course as well if not better than anyone in the field. While attending college at nearby Stanford between 1967 and 1971, Watson made frequent pre-dawn runs to the famed course. Family friend Ray Parga was the starter during Watson's collegiate years and often saw to it that the young Watson, who would often travel solo from Stanford to Carmel, would get an early slot. Additionally, a handful of times a year, members of the team would organize trips to Pebble. After leaving Stanford early in the morning, the youngsters would play two laps around the famed course, playing the closest 9-10 holes from The Lodge. The experience seemed for naught: Watson's failure to register a single under-par round in the '72 Open marked the beginning of what would become a tortuous Open slog.

The next year, when Johnny Miller was rewriting golf history with a final-round 63 at Oakmont, Watson missed the cut. His Open frustration came to an early boil in the mid-1970s, starting with the 1974 Open at Winged Foot. This particular Open, contested on the club's vaunted West Course, set the standard for modern-day Open difficulty. Dizzying green speeds, severe undulations, and jungle-like rough earned this particular championship a permanent place in the annals of U.S. Open sadism. For the entire week only eight rounds broke par. In the first four holes of round one, Jack Nicklaus took 11 putts on his way to a 75. The Westchester County air was rife with complaints and criticisms. In a rare moment of unity both players and media cried foul on the USGA. In fact, one of the most memorable golf quotes ever uttered was spoken that Thursday afternoon in a haze of finger-pointing and frustration. Sportswriters, having gotten a daylong earful from addled contestants, sought out Sandy Tatum, then head of the USGA Championship Committee. Their question to the man who was responsible for the silicon-slick greens and cabbage-like rough: Are you trying to embarrass the best players in the world? Tatum's disarming reply: "No, we're trying to identify them."

Through three rounds of that Open gauntlet, Watson held a one-shot lead over Hale Irwin and a two-shot edge over Arnold Palmer. It's hard to imagine Watson as an unproven entity, but in June 1974 he was winless in three and a half years on tour. Words like "potential" and "future" which had so optimistically framed his arrival on the circuit had begun to weigh heavily. He had developed a reputation as a powerful if wild driver of the golf ball, an excellent chipper and putter, but a poor closer. His 79 in the final round at Winged Foot, the fifth-worst score of the day, did little to raise his confidence.

Afterward, Watson licked his wounds amid the drab metallic lockers inside the stately Winged Foot clubhouse. To his friend and fellow tour player, John Mahaffey, Watson was bemoaning the lack of tempo that had cost him the Open, when in walked Byron Nelson. In addition to 52 tour titles Nelson had won five major championships, including the 1939 U.S. Open. He was a living legend. Since 1957 Nelson had been working as a color analyst for various networks' golf telecasts. With ABC Sports broadcast of the '74 Open bloodbath complete, Nelson sought out the vanquished. He didn't know Watson well (they had only met a year earlier) but that didn't matter. He had been following Watson's career and thought he could help.

As Nelson recalled the scene in his 1993 autobiography, he ordered Watson a Coke and told him, "Tom, I'm sorry you had such a bad day. I've seen quite a few people who've been in the lead but did not play well the last round until they had a few tries at it."

According to Nelson's account, Watson was still pretty down, "which was natural, but he was nice and very polite to me and thanked me for what I'd said. When I left, I told him, 'I'm not working with anyone right now, and if any time you'd like me to work with you, I give you permission to call me. No one else has that privilege."

Two weeks later, fueled largely by Nelson's confidence in him, Watson landed his first professional win. At that time the Western Open, then contested at the brutishly difficult Butler National Golf Club outside Chicago, was still afforded "fifth major" or at least near-major status due its illustrious history and its fading claim as the golf championship of the western United States. The victory legitimized Watson as a Tour player. The next year, 1975, Watson would not only win the Byron Nelson Golf Classic, but he would snare his first British Open in a playoff over Jack Newton at Carnoustie.

But in June, at the 1975 U.S. Open at Medinah, Watson took two steps back. After going 67-68 in the first two rounds for an opening 36-hole record 135, Watson all but evaporated, ballooning to rounds of 78-77 on the weekend. Remarkably, come Sunday afternoon, Watson was still in contention. In fact, he stood on the tee of the 17th hole Sunday knowing a birdie-birdie finish would win and a birdie-par finish would assure him a spot in a playoff. He bogeyed both holes.

The bloodletting continued. In the run-up to the 1979 Open at Inverness, Watson, who had won four of his previous seven tour starts, arrived in Toledo as the prohibitive favorite. He couldn't deliver, laboring instead to sloppy rounds of 75-77 and missing the cut. "I was embarrassed out there," he said.

Clearly there were two Watsons at work: one was stockpiling green jackets, claret jugs and tour titles and the other couldn't get out of his own way in a U.S. Open. For the first Watson—the winning Watson—his momentum would evolve into full-fledged liftoff. He emerged as the greatest player in the world. Between the end of the 1974 Open and the beginning of the 1982 Open he would win 30 times including three British Opens and two Masters titles. But the other Watson remained an Open question: He was 0-fer the Open. Would he—could he—win the national championship he craved? "I had an opportunity in '74 and '75 to win both and didn't finish the deal," said Watson. "I hadn't learned how to win yet. I just wasn't a very accomplished winner. I worked as hard if not harder at the game than anyone else on tour to be my best. The Open just got in my way a couple of times and I just couldn't seal the deal."

Watson's inability to close eventually rendered him untouchable among U.S. Open prognosticators. As the 1982 championship approached, Watson, the top-ranked player in the world, couldn't get a bone. Ben Wright, who would go on to a long career as a CBS Sports commentator (before being dumped by the network in 1996 for an ill-advised comment about LPGA players' breasts) was in 1982 a columnist for *Golf World* magazine. He handicapped the upcoming U.S. Open at Pebble Beach on a points system he had devised for the publication. Jack Nicklaus was Wright's odds-on favorite with 525 points; Lanny Wadkins was next at 200; Raymond Floyd at 190 was followed by Wayne Levi (155) and Tom Kite

(145). George Burns and Tom Watson earned scant notice from Wright, who awarded them 125 points each with Watson earning only 5 points for "current form."

Wright wasn't alone. In June of 1982 there were plenty of people wondering if Watson would ever win an Open, including Watson. A few days before Pebble, he commented on the difference between playing in the U.S. Open, where he was infamously winless, and the British Open, which he had already won three times. "It's (The British) a vacation, the pressures just aren't the same as the U.S. Open. If, when I'm in the twilight of my career and still have not won that (U.S.) title, then I'll worry about it. I'm still young."

Yet even as Watson expressed strained optimism about his U.S. Open future, he had real doubts about his current chances as he arrived on the Monterey Peninsula. He was a basket case. In fact, he felt he had no shot at the '82 Open title. "I knew I had no chance to win because I was hitting the ball sideways. I don't mean sideways, I mean sideways. The only thing I had going for me was that I was so far off-line on a lot of shots that the ball was landing outside the ropes where the gallery had walked, and I was getting decent lies."

If Watson's confidence in himself had eroded, Byron Nelson's confidence in Watson hadn't budged. The two had only grown closer in the eight years since Watson's meltdown at Winged Foot. In search of some last-minute counsel from his 70-year-old friend and mentor, Watson visited Nelson on the latter's Texas farm only a few weeks prior to Pebble. Nelson, who was perhaps the gentlest and most thoughtful man in a sport that has more than its share of egotists, told a reporter at the time that "the only thing on his (Watson's) mind right now is winning at Pebble. Every shot he hit when he was here was designed to work on some hole there (Pebble). If I know

Tom Watson, he will be hard to beat there."

Somewhere in between Nelson's optimism and Watson's crumbling confidence lay the truth.

CHAPTER 9

Fear at the Summit

MORE SO THAN A MASTERS TITLE, a U.S. Open triumph is the pinnacle of performance. Every major championship has its merits, but the U.S. Open carries with it more than the imprimatur of America's national championship: It's the hardest championship to win. Tony Lema, the techni-colorful, high-living star of the mid-1960s who climbed from a childhood on welfare to a berth among the finest players in the game, succinctly addressed the unique challenges of the Open in his 1965 book, *Golfer's Gold*. His chapter about the Masters (in which he finished runner-up in 1963) is tellingly entitled "Fun at the Summit." In it he writes, "The Masters is fun. The stakes are high, of course, the pressure to win is great, but the pleasure of playing in a tournament on the Augusta National is so acute that it almost completely wipes out the pain or nervous tension." By contrast, Lema's later chapter about the U.S. Open is titled "Fear at the Summit." "The difference," Lema writes, "between the Masters and the U.S. Open is the difference between fun and fear. (In the U.S. Open) the greens are slick and fast, the sand traps are as wide and as deep as bomb craters, the fairways are so narrow you could use them to conduct a sobriety test and the rough alongside each fairway and around each green is jungle deep … You can feel Open tension so strongly that it's with you from the very minute you come into town for the tournament until two or three days after it's over. You can feel the tension in a shortness of breath, in a lack of appetite, restless nights and an overpowering desire to drink yourself to sleep in the evening."

Not surprisingly, Lema, who died in a plane crash in 1966, never won a U.S. Open.

The core of the Open's toughness lies not only in the selection of the host course (there are no pitch-n-putts in the U.S. Open course rotation), but also in the manner in which that course is prepared by the USGA. Often referred to as an "Open set-up" this tradition of long holes, narrow fairways, deep, thick rough and hard, fast greens might better be referred to as a "USGA set-up" because the USGA adopts those characteristics not only for the U.S. Open, but for the vast majority of the national championships it oversees (U.S. Amateur, U.S. Women's Open, U.S. Senior Open, etc.).

The idea of toughening golf courses for championships goes back a long way. It's who does the prep work that has changed. From the time the first U.S. Open was played in 1895 until well into the 1950s, the host courses themselves—not the USGA—took responsibility for the set-up of the golf course (This might explain the fact that during the first U.S. Open in 1895, in Newport, Rhode Island, there were reports of worm-castings on the greens). According to former USGA executive director David Fay, it was only after Robert Trent Jones' monstrous re-design of Oakland Hills for the 1951 Open and the "hay" scandal of the 1955 Open at Olympic "that the USGA took the reins" from the host clubs.

Jones' preparation of the south course at Oakland Hills

(begun in 1949) set the standard for mid-century U.S. Open masochism. While he retained the existing Donald Ross routing he tweaked virtually every hole, whether with a re-bunkering here, a new green there, or modifying the surrounds of the trademark Ross putting surfaces. The term "target golf" has since evolved into a pejorative, but at the time Jones boasted of having laid out very specific landing areas. Using pincer bunkering and deep rough, he severely narrowed the fairways for bigger hitters and installed multi-tiered greens defended by brutal bunkers. The course is best known by the infamous moniker bestowed on it by 1951 Open champion Ben Hogan, who, after carding an impressive final-round 67 said, "I'm just glad I brought this course, this monster, to its knees." (Hogan's off-the-record comments were a tad more colorful).

If Trent Jones's re-design, which produced an ungodly average score of 76.27, ignited a debate about Open difficulty, the infamous hay at Olympic four years later was the last straw. After pre-Championship concerns that the rough was not growing in at the exclusive San Francisco club's Lake course, the club leadership decided not to cut it at all for an entire month. When USGA boss Joe Dey arrived on the coast for a pre-Championship inspection he found what amounted to an overgrown penal colony and essentially demanded that all rough within 20 feet of the fairway be cut to about five inches. However, in many places throughout the golf course the wider fringes of the rough remained a foot or more in height. Predictably enough, the remaining deep stuff would play a decisive role in the outcome of the Championship.

During his 18-hole playoff with upstart Jack Fleck, Ben Hogan (again) came to the 18th hole trailing by only a stroke. After losing his footing during his swing, Hogan pulled his drive into the infamous foot-high hay and took three shots to get back to the fairway. He would lose the playoff by three shots. Hogan was not alone. The hay had claimed plenty of victims that week including a caddie who had laid down a golf bag to help look for a ball and was then unable to find the bag.

CHAPTER 10

"My Name is Bruce Edwards"

IN 1978, WAYLON JENNINGS and Willie Nelson fashioned a pop hit from a country song that warned mothers about the nomadic existence of cowpokes. In "Mamas Don't Let Your Babies Grow Up To Be Cowboys," the recording stars advised parents to make their kids "doctors and lawyers and such." Cowboys, argued Nelson, "never stay home and they're always alone. Even with someone they love."

They might well have been talking about caddies. In a day and age where caddies can earn hundreds of thousands of dollars a year; an era when it's not unusual to find a caddie traveling in a Gulfstream jet with his boss, it's hard to remember just how blue the blue-collar job of caddying really was in the 1970s.

It was (and for most caddies still is) a sweaty mélange of endless work, incalculable travel, moldy motels, outdated cars, cheap beer, and chicken wings. It would hardly seem like the kind of lifestyle to which a smart, middle class New England high school kid would aspire. But that assumption discounts what, for a certain kind of teen, is the enduring lure of the vagabond life, the need for constant movement and increasing independence. For an even smaller set of teens, that wanderlust is matched by an appetite for golf—an innate love of the game—and a high regard for the work of a professional caddie. That was Bruce Edwards.

Edwards was born in Wethersfield, just south of Hartford, Connecticut in November of 1954. In business circles, Hartford has always been known as the locus of the American insurance industry. But in golf circles it was long known as the home of the Insurance City Open. The PGA Tour event, which has gone by several names, including the ink-hogging Canon Sammy Davis Jr. Greater Hartford Open (it's now known simply as the Travelers Championship), has been stopping in the Hartford area every summer since 1952 when Ted Kroll won by four shots over Lawson Little, Skee Riegel, and Earl Stewart Jr.

For the first 32 years of its existence, and throughout most of Bruce Edwards' youth, the Hartford event was known colloquially as "the GHO" and staged at Wethersfield Country Club, a place that lacked the social pedigree of nearby Hartford Golf Club, but prided itself on annually playing host to the finest players in the game. Over the course of its more than three decades as tournament host, Wethersfield christened boldface champions such as Snead, Palmer, Burke, Littler, Casper, Venturi, and Strange.

Edwards' parents, Jay and Natalie, were members of the club, and young Bruce's exposure to the game, to Wethersfield's bag-toting sidekicks and to the glamor of a life on tour, seduced him. He embraced the game and became a good player, in particular a very good putter, but he developed a particular passion for caddying at Wethersfield.

"Part of it was the money," he told John Feinstein for the author's 2004 book *Caddie for Life*, but beyond the money, Edwards had his eye on a bigger prize: the fact that late in the summer the club's more conscientious caddies were rewarded with an opportunity to work the GHO, to caddie for actual PGA Tour professionals.

From the first time that Edwards carried a tour player's bag in competition, he was sold on his future. As he told Feinstein, "I knew it the first time I stepped inside the ropes. I just loved the way it felt." In fact, in the 1973 Marianapolis Academy yearbook each student answered the question "What makes you happiest? Edwards' reply: "Caddying on the PGA Tour."

A month after high school graduation, Edwards, at a friend and fellow-caddie's urging, introduced himself to a then almost unknown Tom Watson in the parking lot of Norwood Hills County Club in St. Louis. It was the second-most famous conversation the duo would ever have, and when one considers the fluid and unpredictable nature of life on tour, the cultural gap that existed at the time between the largely black veteran caddies and a young white interloper like Edwards, odds are it never should have happened.

"You have to imagine the time and place," said one college-educated northeasterner who briefly caddied the PGA Tour in the 1970s.

Culturally, PGA Tour caddie-dom was miles from anything a privileged kid from the northeast could have imagined. On the simplest level—basic communication—there were accents and vernacular to decipher. On a deeper level, there were new worldviews to interpret and new lifestyles to fathom.

"There was definitely a culture shock," said this caddie, who ultimately opted for law school. "There were alcoholics, guys who were chasing babes so hard and so constantly it was kind of disgusting. Forget one-nighters, I'm talking about 15 minutes in the Porto-Let. They stunk of booze on the first tee and that was on a good day."

It was this culture into which Edwards, the intelligent son of educated parents (he also happened to have a bit of a grammar fetish) cast his lot. What were the early weeks of a fresh-faced caddie's career in the 1970s like?

"It was like the first week at a new school," said an early colleague of Edwards'.. "Your eyes, your ears, your pores are open to every new sight and sound. You're a little scared and excited, you feel big and small. You'll remember this day forever, but virtually no one you talk to that day will, including the player whose bag you may carry for the next week or so."

The weekly mating ritual of itinerant caddie and needy player was and still is an informal, hit and miss affair. That's because no matter where an eager caddie-to-be hangs out—the parking lot, the practice range, the rest rooms, the hotels—all 50 players looking for caddies that week are unlikely to walk past you. It's not as though they all arrive at the clubhouse at the same time at the same door. Furthermore, "you won't even know half the guys' faces. You could be approaching an agent, a brother, or worse yet, a current caddie about getting that bag."

The greatest asset to a caddie in search of a loop was a pair of coveralls issued by the current week's tournament. Pitching your services in uniform suggested credibility and experience, it greased the skids towards getting a bag for the coming week.

After bouncing around from bag to bag on the 1973 Tour for a month or so, Edwards headed to the tour stop in St. Louis on the prowl. That Tuesday morning he and Watson were a perfect match: Edwards, a bushy-haired, intelligent, polite, out-of-work caddie, and Tom Watson, a bushy-haired, intelligent, polite, and underperforming (read winless) 23-year-old tour professional.

At the urging of friend and fellow caddie, Neil Oxman, Edwards approached his prey saying, "My name's Bruce Edwards. I just finished high school in Wethersfield, Connecticut, and I'm going to spend a year on the tour caddying. If you don't have a caddie right now, I'd like to work for you."

Watson described himself at the time as "a long-haired golfer coming out of the locker room ... and he was a long-haired caddie. We fit the bill together right there."

Famously, the duo agreed to try the arrangement for a week. It lasted 30 years. While the team enjoyed enormous competitive and financial success, their relationship would vastly transcend that of employer-employee. In an age when caddie-player relationships were defined by impermanence, Watson and Edwards were a team, an archetype. They would virtually become family.

Fellow veteran PGA Tour caddie Greg Rita was among Bruce Edwards' closest friends. When asked prior to his passing in 2010 about the key to Watson-Edwards' success, Rita zeroed in on a single word: Loyalty. "Now, caddies are the scapegoats if things aren't working out or if a player isn't playing well," said Rita. "That's because now, with all the money that has come into the sport since Tiger, it's big business."

"What made Tom and Bruce," he said, "was the fact that they were good friends and had respect for one another. That and loyalty and Bruce's exuberance and his confidence in his own ability allowed him to say what he wanted. Tom believed in Bruce. That rubbed off on his own ability. So much of being a good caddie is not being afraid to be wrong. Bruce didn't make many mistakes, but he wasn't afraid to be wrong.

Bruce had such confidence and Tom could feel that and feed off that."

Until the duo of Woods and Williams came on the scene in 1999 (Woods's first tour caddie, Fluff Cowan, was fired after the 1996-1998 seasons) Watson and Edwards were by any measure—titles won, money won, friendship developed, loyalty inspired—the most successful player-caddie partnership in the history of professional golf. There were higher profile loopers, but Nicklaus' Angelo Argea, Gary Player's Rabbit Dyer, and Lee Trevino's Herman Mitchell all came and went while Watson and Edwards plowed on, eventually winning some $8.5 million and more than 30 titles together.

By June of 1982 Edwards, who had struggled with attention deficit disorder as a schoolboy, and who passed on college despite managing 1,130 on his SAT, found himself alone atop his profession. He was working for the best player in the world, living his childhood dream, and making a very nice living. But the pinnacle of professional success, the winning of a major championship, had eluded him. It's not that Watson wasn't winning majors; by the spring of 1982 he'd already won five, it's just that by dint of a remarkably odd combination of history and circumstance Edwards was not on the bag for any of them.

Watson's first major was the 1975 British Open at Carnoustie. Edwards' failure to get a passport in time precluded him from making the trip, so Watson, playing in his first Open Championship, took on a local looper by the name of Alfie Fyles. Remarkably, Watson won in an 18-hole playoff over Jack Newton.

Edwards' next major miss was the 1977 Masters, which Watson won by two shots over Nicklaus. There, Watson had no choice but to abandon Edwards: Until 1983, Augusta National's rules required Masters contestants to hire club caddies. Later that year Watson won the 1977 British Open in a glorious and storied showdown, again with Jack Nicklaus. But Edwards didn't make that trip either. Alfie Fyles was on the bag because the previous year (1976) Watson-Edwards had badly missed the Open Championship cut and Edwards simply couldn't justify the cost of a repeat trip.

Fast forward to the 1980 British Open at Muirfield. Based on the success of the Watson-Fyles pairing in 1975 and 1977, both Watson and his then-wife, Linda, felt an obligation to bring in Fyles again for the 1980 edition. Of course, Watson won again. And in his final major championship win before the 1982 U.S. Open at Pebble Beach, the 1981 Masters, Augusta's rule again forbade Edwards from working the tournament. As Edwards said in Feinstein's book, "There were times when I thought about nicknaming myself the Black Cat, but Tom wasn't even thirty yet, and I knew he was going to win more majors."

There were plenty of close calls for the duo, particularly in the elusive U.S. Open, but for all of their accomplishments they had yet to celebrate together at the pinnacle of the profession. As they arrived at the 1982 U.S. Open, they were already one of the truly great tandems in golf history and well on their way to re-defining the player-caddie paradigm. The strength of their relationship was so great and their success so formidable that only a major championship could improve on that bond, and as the golf world would so bitterly find out in 2004, only Bruce's tragic death could break it.

CHAPTER 11

The Ultimate Penultimate

SIMPLY BY VIRTUE OF ITS LOCATION and its position in the ebb and flow that is 18 holes, a 17th hole ought to be a special place. Regardless of the golf course, the 17th is the high note before the bass finale, the kiss before dying. Shiploads of high-grade ink have been spent in praise of closing holes, but if you were to ask a devout player to choose between just about any 17th hole and any 18th hole, he'd inevitably pick 17 (because the truly devout have faith that 18 will always be there waiting).

If a 17th hole represents the sweetness before the bitter end, there is no sweeter 17th than at Pebble Beach. There are plenty of contenders: The view from the tee box at nearby Cypress Point's penultimate hole is enough to break a heart already strained by the inimitable 16th (not to mention the beguiling 15th). The 17th holes at the Old Course, at Baltusrol's Lower Course, The Olympic Club, Winged Foot (West), are all time-tested treasures that have borne the steely spikes of history. The 17th at TPC Sawgrass is sweet in an ex-wife sort of way. But for the same reasons that Angelina Jolie has it all, the 17th at Pebble Beach is the whole package. Winged Foot's treacherous 17th may have that trademark raised green and a lovely if non-indigenous orange tulip tree thrown in for looks; Sawgrass has its balata-lined lake seemingly clawed out of the mud by Pete Dye's bloodthirst, but neither is a match for a roiling Pacific squall. The 17th at Pebble is an all-you-can-handle buffet, a sensory overload of wind, water, rock, grass, sand, and history.

There's the salty air of Monterey Bay, which hints not only of the incalculable gallonage lurking beyond the green, but beckons the imagination in a way that a landlocked hole simply can't do. That the human body contains about seven teaspoons of salt may explain how a devilish seaside par-three specifically designed to embarrass us can also make us feel at home. The splash of the waves on the rocks behind the green suggests a timelessness that conflicts with that ephemeral Christmas-afternoon ennui that comes with standing on the 17th tee: The long-awaited moment is both here and nearly over.

If like so many other courses, Pebble Beach's holes had names, the 17th would surely be Cybil. If you've played it a dozen times you've seen a dozen versions. There's the wind-blown 17th; the cold and damp 17th; the calm 17th; the sunny 17th; and the 17th that's shrouded in vernal fog ("June gloom" as the locals refer to it.) There's the downwind 17th, which actually plays much harder than the upwind 17th (because the small green is much harder to hold when an insistent off-shore breeze is coaxing the ball seaward). There's the AT&T 17th which shows up every February, shorn of deep rough and fast greens (and featuring shorter tees). And then there is the hole's ultimate incarnation: the U.S. Open 17th, which rears its angry head every decade or so to re-establish the impotence of all but the greatest players in the world.

For all of its deceit and ferocity, the 17th hole is the per-

Chris Millard

fect reflection of Pebble Beach's crazy-quilt history, the product of a unique combination of intricate planning and seat-of-the-pants serendipity.

As mentioned earlier, for the first few years of its life the golf course at Pebble Beach was like an ugly daughter being thrust into marriage by an eager father. Each time Pebble hosted a significant event, the complaints and the qualifiers would roll in: The fairways were too rocky, the conditions were primitive. This would be an issue for the course well into the 1970s and '80s.

"The greens were crap in both 1972 and 1982, said former USGA senior executive director Frank Hannigan. "Pebble was not well maintained until Teddy Horton went there as superintendent in 1993." But Samuel Morse never relented, ultimately landing the 1929 U.S. Amateur.

In a pre-championship review of his work on Pebble Beach in anticipation of the 1929 U.S. Amateur, Chandler Egan was very specific as to the changes he'd made throughout the golf course. With regard to the 17th hole, Egan reported that "a new championship tee has been built back of the road, making a distance of 225 yards. A large double green more or less surrounded by sand dune bunkers has been built on the site of the old green. The left, or 'championship,' half of the green is guarded in front by sand and is separated from the other half by a long ridge. The entire green is particularly visible."

What is known is that Egan's impact on 17 and on the broader golf course was not subtle. He distinctly changed both the look and strategy of Pebble Beach. He planted pantagruelian dunes-like bunkers which dwarfed putting surfaces at holes such as the 17th. He lengthened the course over 200 yards. The course we know today, the course played in

U.S. Opens, Amateurs, and Women's Amateurs since 1929, remains Neville and Grant's routing (with exception of the new Jack Nicklaus 5th hole circa the 1990s), but from a look and feel standpoint the course is the indisputable handiwork of Egan. If one compares the towering height of Pebble's reputation to the minimal credit Egan has enjoyed, a case can be made that he is the most overlooked, under-appreciated architect in the history of the game.

Why the credit for Pebble Beach still sloughs so readily off Egan's reputation is a bit of a puzzler. Approximately 80 years later, in an era when the work of storied designers is routinely erased by shopping malls or by quicky architectural makeovers, the Pebble Beach bylines of Neville and Grant survive in boldface. The roots of that durability lay primarily in their local ties. First, Neville and Grant enjoyed fabled standing as local amateur competitors and there was an undeniably marketable romance in a story about local boys making good (Neville was actually born in St. Louis in 1895 but moved to California as a young boy. Grant was born in New York, but his family lived in California); Second, beyond his playing days, the real-estate agen Neville was a longtime local presence in the Monterey area (Grant moved away to England soon after the completion of Pebble in 1919 and did not return for over 30 years). Finally, it probably didn't hurt that the popular and respected Neville, who was not only a local golf legend and real estate agent, but also a magazine editor, was in a position to affect Morse's business.

"Neville was so well-liked and so well known, Morse was careful not to make Neville look bad," said golf writer and historian Geoff Shackelford.

On the latter point, Morse was believed to be quite keen. According to Neal Hotelling's history of Pebble, Morse "was apparently intent on preserving the legacy of having selected Neville and Grant, unproven entities." He goes on to cite an October 6, 1928 report in the *Peninsula Daily Herald* that seems designed not only to obfuscate Egan's role but to minimize the breadth of his changes: "Only two or three minor changes will be made in the Pebble Beach links this winter in further preparation for next September's National Amateur Golf tournament."

Like any impresario worth his salt, Morse simply would not allow the facts to get in the way of a good PR story. Hotelling cites a 1960s internal memo in which Morse wrote, "… we employed CE (Chandler Egan) to do a lot of refinements at Pebble Beach, construction of greens, traps, etc., but he made no alteration on the original layout of the holes." Technically true, but misleading. Egan created a distinct work of art, he just did it on an existing canvas.

While Morse stuck to the company line for decades, many students of golf course design today credit Egan, not Neville and Grant, for modern-day Pebble Beach. "Egan re-did every hole in terms of strategy and aesthetics," insists Shackelford. "If you look at the old photos prior to Egan, you get a clumsy, awful-looking golf course."

Post-Egan, the 17th green, which is the heart of the hole, has changed significantly. First, the hourglass shape was far less pronounced in the original design. Prior to Egan, the neck portion used to be much wider. It was not necessarily Redan-like in the old days, but, says Shackelford, it was easier to play the ball from the right portion of the green to the left portion.

With Egan's narrowing of the neck, it's not uncommon for people to play a chip shot from the right side of the putting surface to the left (in fact while playing in the 2009

AT&T Pebble Beach National Pro-Am, PGA Tour commissioner Tim Finchem played just such a shot).

Also, over the decades, weather, mowing lines, and relocated bunker sand have conspired to shrink the green considerably. The putting surface is much smaller now than it was in 1929. The signature hump bisecting the green, though unchanged, now occupies a larger percentage of the overall putting surface and therefore seems more prominent.

Aside from Egan's largely aesthetic changes, the one change that may have had the greatest effect on the playability of the 17th hole was actually intended as a change to the 18th. When in the early 1920s Arthur "Bunker" Vincent convinced Samuel Morse to build a tee on the rocky beach behind the 17th green in order to assuage the California Golf Association and make the 18th a more dramatic finishing hole, he impacted the playability of 17. The tee created a slight grass buffer between the back of the 17th green and the beach.

Most holes at Pebble Beach, certainly on the back nine, can warrant an entire chapter, but the 17th hole at Pebble is worthy of its own book. It's among the game's loveliest rubbish bins, a place where great rounds and beautiful dreams are dashed on the rocks like so many broken beer bottles. That doesn't necessarily make it a great hole. In fact, iconoclastic design critic and increasingly influential architect Tom Doak argues that 17 is not even a good hole. His premise: If the smart shot is to play into the front bunker, how good a golf hole can you have? In the 2000 U.S. Open, none other than Tiger Woods supported Doak's argument: The last two rounds of that championship Woods intentionally hit the ball in the front bunker. "(At) 17, I was just playing short," said Woods. "If I flushed a 4-iron in there, it might get over the bunker; if not, I knew it would be an easy uphill bunker shot."

Good, bad, or ugly, few holes in golf have produced more drama. In his autobiography, *My Story*, Jack Nicklaus literally confessed to having nightmares about the hole. With a 1:05 p.m. tee time in the final group on Sunday afternoon, Nicklaus was trying to sleep in that Sunday morning. As he repeatedly awakened and dozed off, the Golden Bear had a recurring dream in which the 17th played a starring role. "I arrived at the 17th every time with a comfortable three-stroke lead, but there was no way I could make par there with the cup left of the hump on the green. Finally, I decided to take a bogey and go on to 18."

Nicklaus was not the first or last to be haunted by the hole. As early as August 1929, shortly before the U.S. Am, the *New York Times* described the hole as "terrifying." A few days later, in the first qualifying round of the Amateur, the great Bobby Jones had the first of two meaningful scrapes with the par-three. He pushed his tee shot right of the green. The ball, clearly headed for the bay, struck a fan on the back and bounced onto the edge of the green. Jones chipped and then putted for par. In the first round of match play, Jones would lip out a birdie putt at 17 to halve the hole and head to the 18th 1-down (he would lose the 18th).

The rogue's gallery of 17th-hole victimhood only begins with Jones. In the 1961 Amateur the previous year's runner-up, Bob Gardner, had what *Golf World* magazine referred to as a "harrowing experience." In the third round, 4-down after eight holes to Homero Blancas, Gardner clawed back and was only one down on the 17th hole. Despite calm conditions, Gardner played a 3-wood off the tee and flew the green. In trying to take his stance to play his third shot, Gardner nearly fell off the cliff onto the rocky shore. After finally taking a lunge at the ball, he moved it all of 15 feet. Blancas parred, won the hole and the match.

The 17th gives and takes on a whim. In the final round of the 1972 Open Nicklaus overcame his own worst nightmare. Just as he had envisioned it during his early morning re-rack, Jack came to the 17th hole with a three shot lead over Bruce Crampton. The hole was in a foul mood. It had cost the field 94 bogeys in the first three rounds. Nicklaus turned to his caddie, Paul Latzke, a teacher at nearby Robert Louis Stevenson High School, and said, "Give me the 1-iron." Nicklaus had enough of a lead to play for the pin, which was perched precariously in what has since become known as the Open Sunday position. The Golden Bear was about to put his stamp on the Open with a shot that would go down as his greatest ever. But while many recall the result, few know that it very nearly didn't happen. Don't try this at home, but in mid-swing, a millisecond after he began pulling the club down from the top, Nicklaus sensed that his club face was too closed. Remarkably he ratcheted down his release of the club, applied a square face to the ball and hit what many believe to be his career shot.

Nicklaus couldn't see the ball, which featured the signature altitude of a Nicklaus long-iron, but traced a perfectly crafted un-Nicklausian draw. The ball honed in on the right side of the flagstick, took one hop on the green, collided with the pin and came to rest like a dead fish, five inches away. All this while his playing partner, Lee Trevino, the man who had beaten Nicklaus in a playoff at Merion the previous year, stood helplessly by.

Nicklaus' play that day, capped by his bravura performance on 17, earned him a third U.S. Open title (in wire-to-wire fashion no less); a 13th major championship, which tied him with his life-long idol Bobby Jones, and a congratulatory call from President Richard M. Nixon. The President, cheeks in full jiggle and facts askew, lauded Nicklaus for making birdie at 17 "when the chips were down" (this despite the fact that the world's greatest player came to 17 with a three-shot lead). Perhaps Nixon was projecting: What Nicklaus, in his jubilation, could not have known, and what Nixon surely did, was that earlier that same morning The *Washington Post* ushered a new term into the American lexicon. The paper featured a headline that read "5 Held in Plot to Bug Democrats' Office Here". Watergate was born. Blame the 17th.

As generous as the famed par-three had been to Nicklaus' fortunes in 1972, it was just as stingy five years later. With Nixon out of office and the PGA Championship in the balance, Nicklaus bogeyed 17 on Sunday when a simple par would have put him in a playoff with Lanny Wadkins and Gene Littler.

The tee shot at 17, particularly under Open conditions (longer tees, faster green, deeper rough) and even more significantly under Open pressure, is enough to make your teeth chatter. "It is," said Gil Morgan, who led the insanely difficult 1992 U.S. Open after 54 holes, "one of the toughest shots in golf."

Morgan speaks from painful experience. Over three rounds of the 1992 Open, the 17th was the most difficult hole of the Championship playing to Sisyphean average score of 3.413. In the third round, Morgan dismissed the gallery's chant of "wood, wood, wood" by selecting a 1-iron. After pushing his tee ball into the right rough, he chipped out and two-putted for a bogey that contributed to his 5-over-par 77.

Legendary amateur Harvie Ward was right when he said, "Pebble Beach can be kind to you. It can also be awfully mean." In 1992 a decade after their memorable seaside showdown, Watson and Nicklaus returned to Pebble for the U.S. Open and, playing with Hale Irwin in the first round, returned to the 17th. Watson's tee shot rolled near the back of the jigsaw-puzzle front bunker. He exploded long, chipped close but missed a short putt. Double-bogey 5. Nicklaus' tee shot bounced into an unplayable lie above the rocks. Double-bogey 5. In the second round, Watson salvaged a par but Nicklaus had a bogey. After more than 100 tournament and practice rounds at Pebble Beach, the Golden Bear later acknowledged he had "misfigured" the 17th hole.

The 17th has shined brightly on and badly burned journeymen and luminaries alike. It plays no favorites. In fact, few players in history have been so rudely received here as the most beloved player the game has ever known.

In 1963, when AT&T was Ma Bell, the Clambake was the Crosby, and Jack Nicklaus was still a chubby 23-year-old challenger, Arnold Palmer hitched his pants on the 71st tee. His 2-iron flew the green and landed on the beach. From there he played a provisional. He found his original ball in a small puddle of water atop a large rock, declared the ball unplayable and opted to play his provisional ball on which he carded a double-bogey five (including a penalty stroke). While since 1962 USGA Rules clearly allowed for such a move, a local rule on the Tour at the time called for penalty of stroke and distance in cases of balls in hazards or balls in unplayable lies. Under what were the Tour rules then, Palmer was required to take a penalty, return to the 17th tee and play his third shot. When Palmer completed his round, apparently finishing in a tie for 20th and due $525, he was informed that he had been disqualified for signing an incorrect scorecard. Palmer's streak of finishing in the money in 47 straight events was lost on the shores of Pebble Beach.

This is what the 17th hole does. It reduces kings to beach-combing commoners. Palmer returned the following year for an added dose of humility. The third round of the '64 Crosby was—what else—rainy (weather had been so bad for so many Crosbys that one local haberdashery began selling rubberized knee-high Wellies as "Crosby boots"). Palmer, his receding hair matted in the dampness, played a 3-wood to the right of the green and onto the beach.

His ball settled on the pebbly shore in the chilly give and take of wavelets. The uh-oh squad arrived, replete with USGA officials, rules men, scorekeepers, photographers, cameramen, and even a rogue Irish setter who looked less out of place on a rainy California beach than the world's best golfer. Appropriately, Jimmy Demaret was supplying color commentary for the broadcast. Demaret, formerly a world class player, in fact, the first man to win three Masters titles, was never one to let a little golf get in the way of a few laughs. With his dapper Hollywood wardrobe and walk-on roles in hit shows such as I Love Lucy, Demaret embodied the sports and entertainment casserole that was the Crosby. In 1962, when snow stunningly canceled one round of the Crosby, it was Demaret who offered the line of the week, "I know I had a few drinks last night, but how did I get to Squaw Valley?"

When the cameras cut to Palmer beachside there was a lot of milling about and conversation … and shots. Ultimately, Palmer would take a penalty shot, drop into some water on the rocks, and hit his third while the waves crashed around him. His ball bounced back into the ocean from which he emerged (another 1-stroke penalty). Now laying 4 he hit his next shot into a crevice in the rocks from which he took another unplayable lie. He played his seventh to the edge of the green and got down in two for a sextuple-bogey nine.

As Palmer—the emperor with soggy clothes—stood on that beach, insouciant seals and a shrugging sea seemed to mock him, his golf ball cradled in pebbles and framed by seaweed, Demaret offered this gem: "Palmer on the rocks. His nearest drop is Hawaii."

Photographs by Tony Roberts

CHAPTER 12

The 1982 Open

P.J. BOATWRIGHT'S SET UP for the '82 Open at Pebble was essentially a repeat of his '72 set up, which in many ways put Pebble Beach on the map. Of course, Frank Hannigan added wryly, "What's to set up at Pebble? You just go to the backest tees and hope there's a lot of wind."

Thursday dawned as suggested by Hannigan: windy, gray, and cool. The ever-droll Herbert Warren Wind, who covered the championship for *The New Yorker*, described the early Thursday conditions thusly: "Waking to greet the new day brought on all the delight of rising in Glasgow in December."

The gloomy, breezy conditions combined with one small but eye-catching tweak to set the tone for the four days to come. Tatum, in his set-up of the golf course, called for wispy eyebrows on the bunkers. The feel was decidedly British Open. All of which played directly into Watson's hands ... or should have.

Early returns by two players on opposite ends of the spectrum held even more promise for Watson. The suave 30-year-old Bill Rogers, defending British Open champion, carded an opening-round 70. His 2-under-par performance was matched only by Bruce Devlin. At 44 years old, the Australian's finest years were behind him. A very skilled player who had the misfortune to be born in the era of Palmer, Nicklaus, and Player, Devlin may have been the original poster child for "best player never to win a major." By 1982 Devlin had conceded to the dictates of age and was spending more time in the TV tower analyzing golf for NBC than he was chasing trophies, but here he was, sharing the lead on Thursday.

The course and the conditions screamed for a player like Watson, but he got off to an atrocious start. The Kansan, who had made Pebble a home course of sorts during his time at Stanford, knew better than most that the key to scoring at the famed course was to make birdies early and hang on late. In his opening round of the 1982 U.S. Open, Watson started bogey, par, bogey en route to an outward 37. Just when it looked as though the back nine might get worse—he was 3-over-par with four holes to play—Watson awakened, birdieing three of the last four holes to card an inward 35 for an even-par round of 72. Again on Friday, knowing that the early holes at Pebble are where competitors make hay, Watson carded an outward 38, but reined himself in to shoot 34 coming in for another round of 72 and a 36-hole score of 144.

Larry Nelson, who was paired with Watson in the first two rounds (72-72), said of Watson's wild driving that if anyone else had played from the positions that Watson did on those two days he wouldn't have broken 80. But Watson, who at the time was a supremely good putter, had the flatstick working. He made putts from everywhere. His ball-striking in his opening 72 on Thursday was fair, but his second-round 72 was described by one writer as "just plain awful," and yet Watson, who battled with alignment issues through that round would later insist, "That round won the tournament."

By one estimate—seconded by many who witnessed it—

the 72 that Watson squeezed out on Friday could easily have been 10 shots higher. Watson hit a grand total of five fairways, but he reasoned, "I did what Tom Watson can do, and that's get the ball into the hole." His birdies on three of the closing four holes were proof.

After two rounds Watson stood a distant five strokes off the pace set by Bruce Devlin. It seemed as though Watson's dream U.S. Open victory would have to wait another year. Then came a breakthrough.

During a practice session on the range that afternoon, it occurred to Watson that Friday's spray-fest might have been due to his lifting his arms too quickly on the backswing. Watson calculated that if he could cut down on shoulder movement in order to turn the shoulders more quickly he just might restore his accuracy. After a few drilled shots he quietly said to Bruce Edwards, "I've got it."

"I made a slight swing correction going into the third round," said Watson, "and it gave me the type of swing that I could hit the ball a lot straighter off the tee and more solid shots."

With renewed confidence, Watson climbed into a share of the lead Saturday, taking advantage of idyllic scoring conditions. Overnight rain had softened Pebble's greens. Watson, who himself described the course as "defenseless," shot a 68 to tie Bill Rogers for the 54-hole lead. Watson's ball striking—in particular his driving—which had been a liability in the first two rounds, became a valued asset.

"I went out that day and absolutely striped it," he said. "Hit the ball about as well as I can hit it." Perhaps the high point—the exclamation point—to Watson's Saturday rebound was his birdie on 18. "We both knew that 18 was the biggest hole of the day," said Bruce Edwards. "We knew that a birdie on the 18th would put him in the last group for Sunday, and that's what you want to do. That way you can be the one dictating what's going on."

The birdie at 18 made a statement, possibly to the field, but more importantly to Watson himself. Going into the final round, Watson shared the lead with Bill Rogers. Nicklaus was three back. Watson was again in position to win the Open, but this time would be different. As Rogers himself said about Watson, "He knew it was his time and place."

Thirty-one is not that young. By that age most men have earned at least a laugh-line or two. But at 31-years-old and standing on the first tee at Pebble Beach with the responsibility of introducing the contestants in the 82nd U.S. Open to the gallery and to the television-watching world, fair-faced David B. Fay looked like an altar boy from a Bing Crosby film.

In more recent years, you were likely to hear veteran starter Ron Read's voice intoning the combatants' names, but typically his face was not shown in extreme close-up. In 1982, Fay's fourth year at the Association, he inherited the starter's job (once performed by the legendary Joe Dey). While Fay may have been flattered to take up Dey's megaphone, he didn't look like it. As ABC's camera closed in on him, he took on the look of a youthful peanut in an elephant shop.

Fay, who went on to become the USGA's long-time and highly-regarded executive director, would become a regular and relaxed presence on USGA Championship telecasts, but he recalls the nerves jangling inside him as groups featuring icons such as Jack Nicklaus and Tom Watson paraded through his first tee at Pebble Beach. In fact, Fay recalls that he had grown so nervous about his network debut that he had written down a few lines about each player—name and hometown—on 3" x 5" index cards.

"Saturday rolls around and they give you a bullhorn and I very nervously read my notes into the bullhorn," said Fay, a post-collegiate Harry Potter. He introduced the 12:38 a.m. pairing of Nicklaus and Calvin Peete. Twenty-seven minutes later he announced co-leaders Tom Watson and Bill Rogers. After his national television debut, his assignments for the day complete, Fay ran to a phone and called his father, a curmudgeonly retired ship captain, who was sure to be watching from the family's home in Tuxedo, New York.

"Ya see me, Dad?" Fay gushed.

"Yeah. I saw you. Five lines. You couldn't memorize five lines?," growled the old salt.

Fay wasn't the only one who was nervous. Watson managed to hit the first fairway, but as he, Rogers, and the phalanx of writers, media, scorers, rules officials, and spectators followed, he turned to his caddie Bruce Edwards and said, "You nervous?"

"Real nervous," came the reply.

"Good," said Watson, "'cuz I'm real nervous, too."

Bing Crosby once said of Pebble Beach that it's "like a sleeping giant, through the first seven holes a good player should be under par … because the next eleven holes are going to examine his skills ruthlessly."

Nicklaus started off like a sleeping bear. He bogeyed the 1st hole and parred the 2nd. Galleryites could be forgiven for wondering whether the 42-and-a-half year old had it in him. Just as the doubts began to build, Nicklaus crushed them. He rolled up his sleeves and made five straight birdies, sending out a steady beat of deafening roars—one every 15 minutes or so—that wafted like smoke signals over the golf course. The unmistakable message to Watson, Rogers, and anyone else within earshot: Nicklaus, the greatest player of all-time, was making his move.

While exciting, this was not unexpected by Watson or anyone else. Birdies are readily available on the front nine of Pebble Beach. This is how you win at Pebble. In fact, any player who hoped to contend on Sunday would have to exploit Pebble's less demanding outward half. Nicklaus, to everyone's excitement (and no one's surprise), was now doing precisely that. He had righted himself and played the front nine in 3-under-par. Watson, playing three groups behind Nicklaus, was less impressive. The challenger to Nicklaus' throne played the front in a rather disconcerting even par.

If Watson was going to win, he would now have to do it on the back, on one of the most demanding nines in the game. He would have to play at a level of excellence that, given the pressure, given his opponent, given the difficulty of the course, and given his heretofore-paralyzing desire for the national championship, was virtually inconceivable. His par at 10 was beyond comprehension. He was so far right of and below the green in two that photographers were forced onto the beach in order to get a feasible angle. His chip from the knee-high seaside gunch that only the USGA and God can grow, barely reached the right fringe. Watson promptly drained the 25-footer for par.

"That really got me going," said Edwards. "That was Tom being Tom under pressure. When we walked off the green I said to him 'Let's go! (Nicklaus) made his big run. This is ours.' The look in his eye told me he was really into it."

"Ten was unbelievable," Bill Rogers recalled in an interview several years later. "Even to have found that ball was amazing and then to chop it up onto the front fringe and make the putt, well, that kind of started his heroics."

Watson was on a roll. On the 11th he holed a 22-foot

birdie putt to take a two-shot lead over Nicklaus. The putter was the least celebrated club in Watson's bag that week, but it was possibly the most important. After bogeying Hole 12, he regained a two-shot edge with an impossible 40-foot birdie putt at 14. A thinned wedge shot that barely cleared the front bunker left Watson a breaking 40-foot birdie putt, the kind of putt that even the best practitioners in the game simply hope to get close. Best-case scenario you leave yourself an uphill par putt.

Just before Watson pulled the trigger a nearby leaderboard posted the news that Nicklaus had birdied 15. They were, at least for the moment, tied. Edwards gave his boss what he later described as "the best read I've ever given him."

Herbert Warren Wind, an eyewitness to the ensuing putt and to Watson's entire back nine, wrote in *The New Yorker* that, "halfway to the hole, the ball seemed to pick up speed. It was still moving fast when it dived into the middle of the cup."

Bill Rogers, put it more succinctly: "Humans three-putt from where he was."

What few people realize about that putt, arguably the most important of Watson's U.S. Open career, was that the degree of difficulty was compounded by the fact that Watson's ball had a noticeable smile in it from the previous thinned shot. "That was the putt that won the tournament for me," said Watson.

Watson, who would miss only one fairway on Sunday, was quietly (well maybe not so quietly) hosting one of the great driving and putting exhibitions in major championship history. More importantly, he had absorbed body blows, some initiated by Nicklaus, a few self-inflicted, and he had come up swinging.

"The die was cast," said *Golf World* photographer Jim Moriarty, who was covering Watson's final round for the magazine. "This was just two heavyweights going toe to toe. When Nicklaus birdied that stretch of holes on the front nine, you just knew it was going to come down to these two guys."

After a routine par—if there is such a thing in the final round of the U.S. Open—at the 15th hole, Watson entered the homestretch, the grassy crucible that tests the mettle, the mind, and the game. Watson hadn't missed a fairway in his first 15 holes, but on 16 his tee ball came to rest in a right fairway bunker. The bunker was a relative newcomer, having only been placed there during the renovation of the course for the 1972 Open. And the man who put it there? Sandy Tatum, the elder statesman of San Francisco golf (it's his sage voice that narrates TV spots for The First Tee). Tatum was a dear and long-standing friend of Watson's. In fact, the two have played in countless AT&T Pebble Beach National Pro-Ams together. Now, however, Tatum's sand-filled brainstorm had trapped his pal's ball. As Tatum followed in Watson's gallery along the 16th hole, *Golf World*'s Moriarty sidled up to him and said, "You may have cost your friend the U.S. Open." Tatum's answer was as tense as it was sincere: "I hope not."

Bob Rosburg was a young on-course reporter for ABC Sports that afternoon. Rosburg was not only the 1959 PGA Champion, but a native San Franciscan who knew Pebble as well as anyone. As an announcer, "Rossi" had a predilection for doom. He became famous for grim commentary such as, "He's dead there" or "He's got no shot there." When Watson's drive found a home in Tatum's bunker, Rossi reported in trademark undertaker fashion, "That one's dead. That's in that new bunker, Peter (Alliss). He has no chance at all."

Rossi was dead right. Watson, who, by the way, would

later criticize his friend Tatum's bunker as "unplayable," ended up having to pitch out sideways. Then, with the pin on the front of the green he hit a sloppy, spinless wedge that released all the way to the back edge of the putting surface— three-putt territory. Alliss did his best imitation of Boris Karloff narrating *The Grinch Who Stole Christmas*, giving voice to what most nail-biting onlookers were sensing, "Here's his moment slipping away." But miraculously, unconsciously, Watson lagged a 60-footer through about 10 feet of break. It stopped within a foot of the hole. Bogey was assured. "I have to say that's probably the best putt I've ever made," said Watson of the putt that didn't even go in.

Sure, he made bogey, and it cost him a shot, but it could have been much worse. So, instead of bogging down, the "Huck Finn of the fairways" left the 16th green feeling energized by his save.

CHAPTER 13

The Shot

AS HE HEADED FOR THE 17TH TEE, Watson was tied for the lead. Moments earlier Nicklaus had finished uncharacteristically. His sloppy par at 18 capped off a 3-under-par 69. One of the great aphorisms of modern PGA Tour history is that Nicklaus never missed putts in the clutch; that if you had one putt to make and you could select anyone to play it for you the axiomatic choice would be Jack Nicklaus. Not this time. On this day it was the putter that betrayed the man frequently referred to as the greatest flatstick practitioner of them all. On both 16 and 17 Nicklaus inexplicably left birdie putts short. Then, on the 72nd hole, Nicklaus faced an imminently makeable 15-foot birdie putt, one that could have put meaningful pressure on Watson. Nicklaus not only missed the putt, he ran it an unseemly four feet past, leaving himself a demanding comebacker. After holing out, Nicklaus in a bizarre confluence of frustration and relief tossed his ball into the crowd. As he began to walk off the green, the home-hole leaderboard posted Watson's bogey at 16. Nicklaus was now tied for the lead.

Back on the 17th tee Rogers had the honor. The handsome Texan was the reigning British Open champion and yet, at only 31 years old, his game seemed to have crested.

After being tied for the lead with Watson going into Sunday, the gloveless Rogers was now en route to a 2-over-par 74, his worst score of the week, and a tie for third place. When Rogers was playing well, he was a two-headed monster: he drew the ball off the tee and faded his irons, but in the final round at Pebble Beach, Rogers was fading everything and as a result he was giving up distance and losing pace with the leaders. Still, he commanded the tee at 17, a fact that may have aided Watson.

Not surprisingly, the 17th had played the toughest hole on Sunday. Its history as a graveyard for good rounds is never distant. Watson had his work cut out for him. He needed to play 17 and 18—758 yards in all—in 1-under-par 7. If he did, he would make golf history, not to mention fulfill the Watson family's vision of national championship glory. Par in, and Watson would face Nicklaus the next day in an 18-hole playoff. A wobble here or on 18 and Watson could easily be sucked into the Sneadian vortex of Open despair.

Watson watched as Rogers drew a 4-wood. The tee markers were only a few paces up from the farthest possible setting; the pin tucked by the USGA's P.J. Boatwright was as far back and left as possible. Frank Hannigan, the senior executive director of the USGA was supplying rules commentary for ABC Sports that week and was positioned at the 17th hole on Sunday.

"It was a very hard hole, just as it had been in 1972," said Hannigan in an interview prior to his 2014 death. It was also much harder than it played in the PGA Tour's Crosby, in which contestants often played from the shorter tees. Hannigan estimated the difference—taking in weather, distance, and pin placement at four full clubs. "It was a long iron into a small target," said Hannigan, "and it was chilly."

As thick as the air was with cool Pacific dampness and good old-fashioned tension, this was relatively familiar territory. This was the 137th time Nicklaus and Watson had competed in the same tournament. Nicklaus had long enjoyed the upper hand in those match-ups, with 67 top tens to Watson's 26, but Watson had been carving out an impressive niche against Nicklaus in the majors. This was their 35th mutual major. In the most recent 31 leading up to Pebble, Watson had an average finish of 15th. He had also won five, three of which came directly at Nicklaus' expense. In the same preceding 31 majors Nicklaus had averaged a 10th-place finish and had won six majors, but not one of those titles came directly at Watson's expense. When it mattered most, in the glare of major championship pressure, *mano a mano*, Watson was gaining on Nicklaus. In fact, in every single major that Watson had won prior to the 1982 Open, Nicklaus was in serious contention. In those five majors: the 1975 British Open, the '77 Masters, the '77 British Open, the '80 British Open and the '81 Masters, Nicklaus' respective finishes were 3rd, 2nd, 2nd, 4th, and 2nd). But for all those major successes, Watson's recent Open failures may have been fresh in the usurper's mind.

As Watson confronted his options on the 17th hole, David Fay, having completed his assignment as starter, was killing time Forrest Gump-style. "I've got nothing to do," he recalled, "So I walk over to the scorer's tent at 18 to sit with Tom Meeks." Meeks, a USGA staffer, was then compiling and checking contestants' scorecards. In the early 1980s, in order to insure against the dreaded mistake-by-committee, scoring-tent duty was a one-man job. That way, if there was a mistake, P.J. Boatwright knew whom to go after.

Fay, making the most of his busman's holiday, decided

that he'd pass the U.S. Open Sunday sitting quietly behind "Tee Ball" Meeks and watching the final round on the television monitor in the tent. "So, I open up the flap in the goofy little blue tent to get the view of Carmel Bay and I settle in," he recalled.

In comes Jack Nicklaus. "He's in a great mood and for good reason," says Fay. "He thinks he's won his fifth Open. He signs his card. Doesn't know me from Adam."

Out at 17, Watson strategized with Edwards. Both had studied this hole a million times before, but this was not another carefree Crosby. Mark O'Meara, who with four wins at Pebble, has had as much success there as any player in history points out that, "in the U.S. Open the 17th is much more difficult than it is in the AT&T. In the AT&T, we play from the middle tee, never from the back tee."

Under gray, cool skies, and with a breeze blowing right to left, Watson and Edwards calculated the shot at 209-yards. Edwards, who had now been working for Watson for nearly a decade, had not been on the bag for any of Watson's heretofore five major championships. He wanted one as badly as his boss. As they considered the shot the duo realized they were between clubs. It would either be a 2-iron or a 3-iron. Edwards lobbied for the 3, reasoning that the harder Watson swings the better he tends to play. Watson, on the other hand, was concerned about the need to carry the hole's massive left green-front bunker. The downside of the 2-iron was that when combined with a few teaspoons of U.S. Open adrenaline, it could potentially leave him long and left, which with the pin deep in the back left position, was, well, a place that Rosburg might describe as dead.

Looking on from the gallery were major-worthy notables such as the unrivaled king of golf journalism, Herb Wind, the

elfin golf historian Bob Sommers, and ... Rainbow Man. His
actual name is Rollen Stewart, but if you were a sports fan
in the 1980s, you knew him best as the guy who wore those
rainbow wigs and T-shirts printed with religious references
and biblical citations. On this day his shirt advised viewers,
"Repent. Jesus Saves."

Watson selected the 2-iron and made his brisk, upright
swing. As the ball sailed into the gloaming, he quickly barked
"Down!" Watson and Edwards could only watch as the dim-
pled orb, aided by a draw and urged by the wind, drifted left
and scooted through the green, into the deep wiry fescue between two bunkers. Sure enough, he was long and left.

"And he's over, into the deep stuff," said Jim McKay with
a dismissive, downward intonation that reflected the pes-
simism of the moment. Aside from the nearby beach, this
might be the worst possible leave at the 17th hole. Not only
was he likely tangled in the deep U.S. Open rough, but Watson had broken the cardinal rule of U.S. Open play: thou
shalt not short-side thyself. He was only about 15 feet away
from the pin and playing to a slick green that sloped away
from him. It would all come down to his lie. If it was as poor
as could be expected, Watson's dream of a U.S. Open title would be dashed. And he knew it. As player and caddie
headed for the green, Watson flipped the club to Edwards
and said grimly, "That's dead."

Frank Hannigan was in the booth at 17 doing double duty
for the USGA and ABC. His reaction to Watson's shot was
somewhat more optimistic. "Remember," he added, years
later, "Watson was what Seve was around the greens. So, I
would have thought he had a 50-50 chance of making three."
No mention, however, of making two.

If Hannigan liked Watson's chances of at least making

par, sentiment almost everywhere else had shifted to Nicklaus. It made sense. If Watson was going to settle for, at best,
a par at 17, and more likely a bogey, he had a world of work to
do on 18 and nearly a century of odds against him: No player
had ever birdied the final hole to win a U.S. Open. Nicklaus
himself says that after watching Watson's tee ball hide in the
greenside rough at 17, "I thought it was over. I thought I had
won the tournament." He and about 20 million other people.

ABC was thinking the same thing. In fact, only a few minutes after Watson missed the green, Jastrow dispatched Jack
Whitaker to interview Nicklaus in the scoring tent. Meanwhile, David Fay is watching the tableau unfold before him.

"We're all watching the telecast and we all see where
Watson's ball goes," said Fay. "Jack's beaming, feeling really
good at that point. So Meeks is doing his numbers and stuff,
and Jack Whitaker turns to Jack Nicklaus and they're chat-
ting, and no one is really watching the monitor, except me."

Watson's ball, which lay in a spot where Chandler Egan
had positioned a bunker more than half a century earlier only
to be overruled by the strident Pacific winds, had become the
focal point of the sports universe. Jastrow, directing the telecast for ABC, demanded shots of the lie. The path to the pin
and the location of the ball had become a form of true north
for photographers and cameramen, who would need to lo-
cate the pellet and then assess the best angle from which to
film Watson and his next shot. A herd of writers, rules officials and spectators scurried about.

As Watson, in his dark blue Fila-logoed sweater, blu-
ish-gray slacks and coffee-colored spikes clambered toward
the green, Edwards pre-empted the gloomy conclusion at
which his boss and much of the world had already arrived.
"Hey, let's see what kind of lie we have," he said to his crest-

fallen employer. "We can still get it up and down."

At the moment it must have seemed like the empty encouragement of a friend, but as the duo drew closer to the lie, Bruce glimpsed the ball. "I could see it," he said later. "That meant it wasn't buried completely. Which gave us at least a fighting chance." Suddenly Watson went from thinking "dead" to thinking "life support."

Frequent close-ups on ABC showed that the lie was better than one might have feared. Still the shot required ultimate touch. Watson and Edwards studied. The ball was sitting up quite nicely, high enough that a magician like Watson could probably work a sand wedge underneath. In fact, the lie at 17, though far from perfect, may have been the biggest and most important break of Watson's career. Moriarty, who had been following the Watson-Rogers grouping since about the 6th hole, watched Watson's tee shot. Like everyone else in the media horde, he had assumed on the spot that Watson had just lost the championship. Only after getting up closer to the green did Moriarty and most inside-the-ropes observers realize the irony of the situation: Had this been a Crosby with no real rough to speak of Watson's draw would almost certainly have kicked left and found a place on the beach, but here in the Open the deep rough actually saved him.

"If there's no rough and it kicks left he's gone," said Moriarty.

While Watson managed his nerves and his strategy, Jastrow managed the delicate telecast. By 1982 Jastrow had directed six U.S. Opens. His trademark, a hallmark of Arledge-era ABC Sports, was the extreme close-up.

"Roone taught us that it was not so much the sport as it was the human drama of it, the emotion which really made these telecasts rich," said Jastrow.

The team of Arledge, Howard, and Jastrow pioneered the use of hand-held cameras and "low tight" cameras in golf. But for U.S. Open telecasts, such potentially intrusive cameras required USGA approval. Working closely with Frank Hannigan of the USGA, Jastrow and company were forever pushing the envelope with lenses and camera locations "in order to really get extreme tight shots ... to see inside the face," said Jastrow. "Not only did we show the face, but we showed the grip and the lie and the ball and all of that."

In the 1982 U.S. Open at Pebble the cameraman at the 17th hole was Drew De Rosa. His placement there says as much about his skills as anything. Says Jastrow, "You can imagine that the cameramen on 18, 17, and 16 were the best. THE BEST. And the low cameramen had special skills of being able to really get in there tight." Jastrow ordered Drew "in there tight on face shots, grip, and lie."

Nicklaus was watching on the ABC monitor in the scoring tent. "I figured it would take a miraculous shot to even get the ball within 10 feet of the hole," he said.

He was then interviewed live by Whitaker, who all but handed Nicklaus the trophy. Before sending the action back to Watson at 17, the typically unflappable veteran former CBS announcer, who was in his first ever appearance on an ABC golf telecast, actually said to Nicklaus, "It's a pleasure to be in your time." Both the sentiment and the terminology were awkward, but they clearly reflected the sense, now permeating the ABC production staff, that Nicklaus had already won.

"We all thought he (Nicklaus) had done it," admitted Jastrow. "He had won the Open there in '72 and he had won the amateur there in '61 and ... he had a way of making other people fall away. He did it 18 times in professional majors and we all thought he had done it. When Whitaker did the interview with him to the left of the 18th hole, it was more or less a winner's interview."

Ironically, Nicklaus himself would make a similar gaffe 10 years later in prematurely congratulating Scotland's Colin Montgomerie on his first U.S. Open, only to see Tom Kite play the final nine holes in even-par to win by two shots over Jeff Sluman and by three over the star-crossed Scot.

With regard to Nicklaus, ABC jumped the gun despite precedent. Although no one had ever birdied the final hole to win an Open, Arnold Palmer holed out from beside the 16th green at the 1962 Masters to assure a spot in a playoff with Gary Player and Dow Finsterwald (Palmer would go on to win the playoff). Then there was Lee Trevino's dagger on the 17th hole at Muirfield in the 1972 British Open. Merry Mex's chip derailed none other than Nicklaus, who had the third leg of a Grand Slam, virtually in hand.

Written off or not, Watson was now the last man standing. An operating room-like hush fell over the ABC staff. In tense times such as this, Chuck Howard, the bombastic executive producer actually backed off. "Believe it or not Chuck would get quiet," said Jastrow. "He knew that the director had lots of work to do and needed lots of concentration. He would actually get quiet and actually lean back on the chair, kind of give way."

It was eerily quiet in the mobile unit. To an audience of some six million viewers (this was decidedly not cable) Jim McKay, the narrator-in-chief of American sport, said, "Now comes, well, possibly, the decisive shot of this Championship."

McKay shared the lead announcers' booth with ABC's Dave Marr, the smooth, affable Texan, who was as recognizable for his sense of humor as for his trademark twang. Marr knew something about battling odds and titans. He'd been on both the winning and losing ends of major championship scrapes. In the 1964 Masters, Arnold Palmer basically won wire-to-wire (he shared the first-round lead with four other players), but Marr, playing with Palmer in the last group, had been in relative contention until he dunked his tee-ball at the 12th hole. As the two close friends stood on the 72nd tee with a handful of strokes separating them, Palmer said to Marr, "Is there anything I can do for you?" Marr's pitch perfect response: "Yeah, make a 12."

The next year at the PGA Championship at Laurel Valley Golf Club in Ligonier, Pennsylvania, it was Marr's turn. Palmer would defeat himself—on his home turf no less—finishing 14 strokes off Marr's winning 280 total. But Marr still faced charges from none other than Nicklaus and Billy Casper, who is often overlooked in the annals of the game's great players. On the final hole, Marr hooked his ball into a bunker, played out short of the green-front water hazard and coolly played a 9-iron to 3 feet. He would hole the putt to hold off Casper and Nicklaus by two. It was the only major championship Marr would ever win, and in a sentiment that reflected both fans' and players' affection for Marr, Arnold Palmer described Marr's win as "one of the happiest moments of my life."

Marr's loveable mixture of coolness and warmth made him popular not only with viewers and network brass, but a favorite of young ABC staffers. "Dave Marr really was a mentor to me," said NBC sportscaster Jimmy Roberts, who began his career at ABC. "Chuck Howard was a mentor in that you learned to be better at your job under his pressure, but Dave was a mentor in the old-fashioned sense: he meant to be helpful."

One example of Marr's soothing paternalism unfolded during the 1982 British Open at Troon. Even by British standards Saturday's round was miserably wet and cold. Roberts, the young production assistant, was having a tough time, "not doing so well in my job that week." Saturday's telecast was finally over, Howard had been screaming at him all day. That afternoon, at the end of a long slog, Roberts skulked into the Turnberry Hotel soaking wet. There, in the bar, were the ABC Sports bigwigs: Jim McKay, Jack Whitaker, Chuck Howard, Terry Jastrow, and Dave Marr. "I felt humiliated because I'd had such a bad day," said Roberts. "I was embarrassed. I felt like they were all looking at me thinking 'he's incompetent.'"

Marr spotted Roberts, sent his colleagues on their way and reached out to the young man. "He puts his arm around me, takes me to the bar, orders two scotches and says, 'I know Chuck was a little rough on you today, and it's hard for you to understand right now, but he's only trying to make you the best you can be. Someday you're going to be grateful for him.' It was one of the nicest things anyone's ever done for me," said Roberts. "This was Dave. He was just an extraordinary guy."

And funny, too. Marr died in 1997 at the M.D. Anderson Cancer Center in Houston. Only days before his death he was laying in bed, his sobbing daughter Liz by his side. In between tear-stained heaves, she was bemoaning his demise, saying at one point, "This is the saddest day of my life." This prompted a nearly comatose Marr to open one eye and say to his daughter, "You think this a sad day in your life ..."

With Marr and McKay on the microphones, Bob Rosburg reporting on the ground and Jastrow et al. in the truck, ABC was ready. The moment was here. It was too late for coaching. "All you can do at this point," said Jastrow, "was make all the conditions right and then let it happen. Let the people and facilities respond to capture it."

As he planned his own attack, Tom Watson was in possession of a secret weapon. Throughout his career Watson had modeled himself after Ben Hogan, that is, he'd made a pregame routine of practicing the toughest shots that that day's course could present. If a course had deep bunkers, he'd practice deep bunker shots. Lots of trees, meant low punch shots. Pebble called uniquely for short chips from deep, possessive rough to scary-slick greens.

"I practiced that shot all the time in the practice rounds, knowing that I was hitting the ball really poorly and knowing that I was going to be faced with that particular shot," said Watson.

Bruce Edwards, just like Nicklaus, Jastrow, Marr, and the millions watching at home, knew that even in the best case, even with all Watson's practice, even with his surprisingly decent lie, Watson would be lucky to stop the ball fewer than 10 feet past the hole. Hoping for the best, Edwards offered a piece of rooting advice, and in doing so laid the foundation for the most memorable caddie-player confab in golf history.

"Get it close," said Edwards.

Watson's famous reply: "Get it close? Hell, I'm gonna make it!"

"I said it more out of just trying to get myself ready to play the shot than anything else, mentally play the shot," said Watson. "And when I got up over the ball, I knew what I had to do."

Watson knew that his only chance to hole the shot or even get it close was to hit the flagstick. If not, he, Edwards, Rogers, Nicklaus, and the civilized world knew that on a downhill, triple-cut U.S. Open putting surface, this shot—Watson's 2,889th in U.S. Open play—could easily roll into oblivion.

McKay and Marr, sensing the import of the moment, kept their commentary simple.

McKay: "Now comes, well, possibly the decisive shot of this championship."

Marr: "This is a shot of his that he generally plays very well. Of course, the conditions now that he plays, they certainly test anyone. So we'll just have to see. "

Watson took his stance and waggled. After a swing as smooth as it was abbreviated, the ball, a Golden Ram No. 1, came out as high and soft as standard-issue human nerves would allow. It lifted off the face of the club—a 56-degree Wilson Dyna Power sand wedge salvaged a few years earlier from a cache of castaways in David Graham's garage. Marr eyed the ball and it's every rotation. "It looks good. It looks good," he said in a rising voice filled with possibility. As the ball started toward the hole, it began to take the break. Just before it collided with the pin, Watson crouched slightly and burped out hopefully, "That's in the hole," and as it began its freefall into golf lore, an incredulous Marr asked his audience, "Do you believe it?! Do you believe it?!"

Watson then surprised anxious photographers and cameramen by bouncing onto the green in an exultant jog. Ironically, this rather un-Watson-like expression of unguarded rapture would become the reserved champion's signature moment. He turned and shot Edwards, the game's greatest I-told-you-so: "I told you!! I told you I was gonna make it!"

While the earth seemingly heaved, Bill Rogers stood stunned, motionless on the edge of the green. Remarkably this was not the first time he had experienced Watson's last minute short-game brilliance. In fact, two years earlier, at the

Byron Nelson Classic, Watson had chipped in on the 71st hole to deprive Rogers himself of a victory.

"I've seen him do a lot of remarkable things, but 17 (at Pebble) was shocking," Rogers said years later in an interview for the USGA. "That birdie put me in absolute shock—I'll remember it all my life."

So will Nicklaus. The greatest player in the history of the game had been robbed. The man who only seconds ago seemed to have nine fingers on a fifth Open trophy, had been pistol-whipped by fate. Worse yet, he learned the news not from the sage Whitaker or from his caddie (eldest son Jackie), or even a close friend, but from a tow-headed vagabond USGA staffer named David Fay. Remarkably enough, when Watson's shot found the bottom of the hole neither Nicklaus, nor Whitaker, nor Meeks was watching the monitor in the little tent by the sea. Why should they, the shot was impossible?

But Fay was watching, and when Watson's ball tumbled into the hole he blurted out, "Holy shit, he holed it!" His words pierced the hushed gathering.

Nicklaus spun around in a swivel chair, glared at Fay, and said flatly, "No he didn't."

Fay responded, "Uh, yeah, he did' and pointed to the black and white monitor. "Look."

The screen was filled with images of Watson's balletic celebration. Nicklaus, expression drained from his face, stared at the monitor. "I can't believe it," he said. "I can't believe it happened again."

Nicklaus recalls that "Jack Whitaker was interviewing me and he was just finishing the sentence, 'Jack, it's been a great privilege to cover you in your time.' I could have been the only guy to ever win a fifth U.S. Open. Then there goes the yell. As I turned around, there was the monitor and I see Watson running across the green."

Numerous accounts describe the stunned Nicklaus (who fainted at the first sight of all five of his newborn children) as pale. Fay concurs. "For a moment he was ashen, but, says Fay, "he quickly re-grouped and he was Jack Nicklaus again, the most gracious loser the game has ever seen."

When ABC's Jim McKay caught the image of a pallid Nicklaus watching an era fade, he said to his audience, "Nicklaus, watching our coverage on a monitor, now knows he can't do a thing. A man like Jack Nicklaus doesn't like to stand there helpless."

Watson's work wasn't finished. He only had a one-shot lead, and there was an ocean's worth of water hazard lining the entire left side of Herbert Fowlers' par-five 18th hole. He could be forgiven for thinking about Sam Snead's four second-place finishes in U.S. Opens. Specifically Watson, the student of Open history, could have been reminded of the 1939 Open at Philadelphia Country Club. Snead needed only to par the par-five 72nd hole in order to win, but he inexplicably tripled the hole and handed the title to Byron Nelson. Snead never won an Open.

Then there was the adrenaline. It nearly cost Tiger Woods the Masters in 2005. Who doesn't recall that crazy, heart-stopping Nike-sponsored chip-in on 16? What few recall is that with his pounding heart lodged somewhere in his esophagus, Woods proceeded to the 17th, where he promptly missed the fairway and bogeyed the last two holes.

Watson's method for composure retention was surprisingly vanilla: Simply play the shot at hand. "I had played the hole a number of times in the Crosby. Sure, there was a little more pressure in this one," confessed Watson, "Still, it was the same shot." Watson opted for 3-wood, and "I hit it as solidly and as flush as I could." About 270 yards worth of solid and flush.

They say the strategy for success at Pebble Beach is to make your birdies early and then hang on through the savage back nine, but on this day all the old rules, along with the old order, would go out the window: As Watson strode to the picturesque 18th tee he was 5-under for his last eight holes. A simple par at the last would win, yet Watson would close the deal in style: 3-wood, 7-iron, 9-iron, all capped off by a long birdie putt that dropped in after authoritatively ramming the back of the hole. In fact, moments after capturing the elusive National Open, when Watson called home to wish Ray Watson a most Happy Father's Day, the old man said, "Boy, you don't know how to lag do you?"

The son responded, "It wouldn't have been more than 6 inches by the hole ... "

To which the delighted father responded, "Bullshit!"

Watson had won his U.S. Open. Furthermore, for the fourth time in six years, he'd beaten Jack Nicklaus in a major championship. The Kansan had turned back both the game's greatest player and the inertia of his own expectations. He had become the player he'd dreamed of being. In response to Watson's win, Fuzzy Zoeller captured the sense of personal breakthrough for Watson and what it might portend for his fellow competitors, "Tom Watson has conquered the mind."

Watson wasn't thinking about all that as he celebrated on the 18th green. He couldn't have been thinking much at all when he tossed what was now among the more valuable golf balls in the world into Carmel Bay (Note: One of the balls from the historic round was kept by Edwards and is now back in Watson's possession while the famed sand wedge now resides in a display case at The Greenbrier).

Nicklaus greeted Watson on the 18th green. The slayer and the slayed. While the respect they felt for one another was never diminished and the friendship they share today is genuine, there was an awkward moment in which Nicklaus consciously or unconsciously assumed the role of victor and put his arm around Watson's shoulders. Watson, in an object lesson in body language, quickly re-ordered their arms, assuming the superior, sympathetic position and offering a champion's condolences to the vanquished.

They shook hands and Nicklaus told him "I'm proud of you." Moments later, at the trophy presentation, Nicklaus warmly teased his opponent, "You did it to me again, you little son of bitch," then added, "If it takes me the rest of my life I'm gonna get you one of these times."

It would never happen. One of the game's greatest rivalries was spent. Few would have believed it as the sun set that day, but that duo would never finish one-two in a major again. This was the beginning of the end for Nicklaus' career and the shining moment of Watson's. He once summed it up this way, "That shot, that day, that moment was the highlight of my life as a golfer."

It was the fourth time in six years that Watson had nipped Nicklaus in a major. More importantly, Watson had his U.S. Open title—the only major championship he and Bruce Edwards would ever win together—and he was now the undisputed greatest player in the world.

It was an Open-and-shut case.

EPILOGUE

The Aftermath

THE 1982 U.S. OPEN MARKED the last time Jack Nicklaus seriously contended for a U.S. Open title on Sunday afternoon.

In 1995, the Pebble Beach Company, after a series of changes in ownership, finally re-acquired the Beatty property, the stray 5.5-acre Stillwater Cove parcel that was sold off by an impetuous Samuel Morse in 1915. The price: $8 million. The site was split into three lots and sold to Charles Schwab, the investment broker, and West Coast auto dealer Don Lucas. The third parcel was set aside as the home of the new 5th hole. After consulting with some of golf's most notable names, including Nicklaus, Watson, and Johnny Miller, Pebble selected Nicklaus to design a new 5th hole (and to tweak the 4th and 6th greens).

A few short years after Watson's 1982 Open win, the foundations of his game would begin to crumble. By 1985, the putting stroke that had carried him through the back nine at Pebble—the stroke that made it possible for "The Shot" to even matter—had not only abandoned its master, it had turned on him. Watson put it very plainly in a 1985 interview with *Sports Illustrated*: "It's a matter of being ill at ease with the putter," said Watson. "It doesn't feel good and it doesn't look good to me."

Through much of the remainder of the decade, Watson was a non-factor.

In 1989, as Watson's game continued to falter, Greg Norman approached Edwards about taking up the Australian's bag. Initially Edwards resisted Norman's offer out of loyalty, but Watson generously recommended the move, and Edwards ultimately made it. The ensuing three-year gap was the first for Watson and Edwards in almost 20 years.

In 2002, Edwards, who had been noticeably slurring his words, was diagnosed with ALS by the Mayo Clinic.

In summer 2003, with Edwards dying of ALS but bravely on the bag, 53-year-old Watson briefly took the opening round lead and made the cut at the U.S. Open at Olympia Fields.

One month later, Watson competed in the 2003 British Senior Open at Turnberry. Bruce was unable to make the trip. Edwards had said to Watson, "You're going to go over there and win the British Senior Open without me." Watson corrected him. "I'll do it for you, pal." He did.

In late 2003, Watson wins the Champions Tour's season-long Charles Schwab Cup, earning a $1 million bonus. He donated the entire sum to ALS research.

At 6:26 on the morning of April 8, 2004—Thursday of Masters week—Bruce Edwards dies. Watson was informed in the Champions' locker room at Augusta National. In a press conference that day, an emotional Watson said angrily, "Damn this disease."

Since 1982, ABC Sports has been reduced from the paragon of sports broadcasting to a bit player. ESPN is the uncontested leviathan. The practice of airing ABC Sports on ESPN—which was so offensive to ABC staffers of the 1980s—is now commonplace.

At the end of 2007, after a re-shuffling of PGA Tour broadcast rights, ABC largely dropped golf.

Golf Digest began ranking the Top 100 courses (originally listed as the Toughest Courses or Tests) in 1985. In 2001, for the first time in its history, Pebble Beach attained the Number 1 ranking, at least temporarily displacing Pine Valley.

Beginning in the late 1990s, Nicklaus took an extended farewell tour of the major championships. His final goodbye came after the second round of the 2005 British Open. Nicklaus birdied his closing hole, but missed the cut. His pairing partner that day, and among the first people to embrace the newly retired Golden Bear: Tom Watson.

After 1982, Watson would never win another U.S. Open. He rocked the world in 2009, when at age 59 he came within an eight-foot putt of winning a sixth British Open title.

A few months after his 1982 U.S. Open win, Watson returned to Pebble Beach for a celebratory dinner with friends, Robert Trent Jones Jr., former USGA president Sandy Tatum, and Hank Ketchum, the cartoonist who created "Dennis the Menace." As the conversation bounced around, Watson quietly exited the restaurant and returned with a handful of golf clubs and golf balls. He proposed to the group a midnight excursion: a return to the 17th hole. By the light of the moon, they found the hallowed spot. As Watson tried his hand at recreating history, he skulled the ball over the green.

BIBLIOGRAPHY

Caddie For Life: The Bruce Edwards Story, by John Feinstein
How I Played the Game: An Autobiography, by Byron Nelson
My Story, by Jack Nicklaus with Ken Bowden
The Architects of Golf, by Geoffrey Cornish and Ron Whitten
The U.S. Open: Golf's Ultimate Challenge, by Robert Sommers
Fifty Years of Golf in America, by H.B. Martin
Pebble Beach Golf Links, The Official History, by Neal Hotelling
The Official U.S. Open Almanac, by Sal Johnson
Golf World magazine
Sports Illustrated
The New York Times
PGA Tour transcripts
Pebble Beach website, www.pebblebeach.com

Interviews
Tom Watson
Jack Nicklaus
Jimmy Roberts
Ben Harvey
Terry Jastrow
Keith Gunther
Steve Anderson
Frank Hannigan
David Fay

Jim Moriarty
Sal Johnson
Charles Millard
Maureen Millard
Mary Cummings
Geoff Shackleford

Additional Resources
ABC Sports (1982 U.S. Open Championship footage)
Golf Channel (Tom Watson interviews)
Assorted San Francisco area newspaper archives
Golf World Magazine archives
Golf Digest archives
Sports Illustrated archives
New York Times archives
USGA archives
"Sandy Tatum: An Oral History," courtesy of the USGA
Tournament transcripts

Special Thanks
Barry Hyde

ABOUT THE AUTHOR

NEW YORK TIMES-BESTSELLING AUTHOR Chris Millard is a veteran observer of the American sports scene. He has covered golf as an editor and columnist at *Golf World* Magazine and as an executive editor at GOLF Magazine Properties. His work has appeared in *Golf Digest* and the *New York Times* and has been recognized on five occasions by the Golf Writers Association of America (GWAA). In 2012 he was awarded the GWAA's first prize for magazine feature articles for his retrospective on the 1986 Masters.

In addition to his work as a sportswriter, he has been a contributor to Golf Channel and served for several years as director of communications for Jack Nicklaus. His books include: *Nicklaus By Design: Golf Course Strategy and Architecture* (with Jack Nicklaus, 2002), *Golf's 100 Toughest Holes* (2004), *Awesome Bill From Dawsonville* (with Bill Elliott, 2006), *My Life Was This Big ... And Other True Tales From a Fishing Life* (with Lefty Kreh, 2008), *The Golf Book: Twenty Years of the Players, Shots and Moments That Changed the Game* (2014), and *The National Golf Links of America: A History* (2017).

A New York-area native and a graduate of the College of the Holy Cross, he resides with his wife and two children in Atlanta and spends summers in Connecticut.